TRANQUILITY

TRANQUILITY

Pathways to Inner Peace

By the author of
A New Day, At My Best,
and *A Time to Be Free*

BANTAM BOOKS
NEW YORK • TORONTO • LONDON • SYDNEY • AUCKLAND

TRANQUILITY

A Bantam Book / November 1993

Library of Congress Cataloging-in-Publication Data

Tranquility : pathways to inner peace / Anonymous.
       p.   cm.
   Includes index.
   ISBN 0-553-37035-9
   1. Peace of mind.   2. Peace of mind—Religious aspects.
BF637.P3T73   1993
158'.1—dc20   93-18822
                                                                    CIP

Published simultaneously in the United States and Canada

Bantam Books are published by Bantam Books, a division of Bantam
Doubleday Dell Publishing Group, Inc. Its trademark, consisting of
the words "Bantam Books" and the portrayal of a rooster, is Registered
in U.S. Patent and Trademark Office and in other countries.
Marca Registrada. Bantam Books, 1540 Broadway, New York,
New York 10036.

PRINTED IN THE UNITED STATES OF AMERICA

FFG   0 9 8 7 6 5 4 3 2 1

Contents

TRANQUILITY

1

Introduction:
From Turmoil to Tranquility

Not long ago, during spring vacation, I took my ten-year-old nephew and his friend to Disneyland. Although we started out early enough, the traffic was stop-and-go most of the way. What should have been a forty-five-minute trip took more than two hours.

The parking lot was jammed when we finally arrived. As the boys and I joined the throng of people flooding toward the entrance gates, I began to have serious misgivings about the outing. My attitude deteriorated even further once we were inside. I fretted about the boys' getting lost; it was impossible to get from one place to another without weaving through endless clots of people.

There were long lines for everything—food,

souvenir shops, and especially the rides. By the time we were in line for our first ride, Pirates of the Caribbean, my stomach was churning.

None of this seemed to bother my nephew and his friend; they remained excited and full of youthful energy. I, on the other hand, was completely unnerved. My character defects flared; I soon became impatient and judgmental of everything and everyone. At one point, I berated a young mother and her two children who had unwittingly cut into the ice-cream line in front of us.

By day's end I had a throbbing headache and a bad case of indigestion. I was so irritable that the boys cautiously kept their voices down. I hardly spoke to them on the way home. All I could think about was how miserable I felt and how stressful the day had been.

At home, when I had calmed down, I felt embarrassed and regretful. The day had been really important to the boys, yet from morning to night all I had thought about was myself.

My inner disquiet brought me back to the life I had led years earlier, when every day was marred by roller-coaster emotions. I plunged from euphoric highs to abysmal lows, anxious and edgy, always ready to explode. I was at odds with everything around me—people, places, things. More than anything, I was at odds with myself. My constant inner turmoil caused me chaotic days and sleepless nights.

Remembering what life used to be like, I felt grateful that experiences such as the one I had that day at Disneyland are now few and far between. Most of the time these days, come what may, I have a deep sense of serenity. I'm at peace with myself and the world around me.

What Is Inner Peace?

· *To know inner peace* is to be in harmony with the world around us, no longer in conflict with our fellows and surroundings, but flowing along with life's natural order.

· *To know inner peace* is to have vision unclouded by anger, confusion, and fear—seeing things clearly, as they truly are.

· *To know inner peace* is to have faith that everything is as it should be, not only the obviously good, but also the seemingly bad. It is believing that every occurrence has a purpose and is part of a Divine plan.

· *To know inner peace* is to live authentically, in accordance with our true selves, free of social pressures with no need for posturing and pretensions, motivated by our hearts rather than our minds.

· *To know inner peace* is to venture into the world confident and unafraid, free of the past; living without guilt, resentment, or blame; present in the here and now, with the desire and capability of living each moment to its fullest; a friend to one's self, comfortable and serene even in solitude; satisfied with what we have been given, and grateful for life.

Deep, abiding tranquility—isn't this what most of us have yearned for throughout our lives? Haven't we all thought, hundreds of times, "I'd give anything for just a moment's peace!"

Perhaps, in the back of our minds, we felt it was an impossible dream. We were too high-strung, too emotional, too scarred by past experiences, too undeserving. Or there were too many outside pressures in our lives—financial burdens, family responsibilities, career demands.

But such reservations, however persuasive, usually aren't enough to stop people from pursuing peace of mind. Some seek it in brain-numbing substances—alcohol, drugs, or food. Some turn to other people, in the belief that the right relationship can be the answer. Some believe that solace will finally come with a certain level of material gain—money, property, prestige. And some feel that a geographic change—to another house, city, state, or country—is the key.

In my own case, I traveled down all of these

avenues—as well as some others—in a desperate search for inner peace. Each new dependence assuaged my inner turmoil for a time. But sooner or later I ended up feeling, once again, trapped and spiritually bereft—overwrought, overwhelmed, and fearful.

The reality, of course, is that true and lasting inner peace can never be found in external things. It can only be found within. And then, once we find and nurture it within ourselves, it radiates outward.

Take a moment to think about people you have known who are at peace with themselves and the world around them. A former teacher, a tennis partner, or someone at work may come to mind. There's something special about such people—it's evident in their facial expressions, their tone of voice, their body language, and, above all, in the way they interact with others. No matter what is going on, they are able to respond with grace while bringing assurance to others.

You respect such people and are drawn to them; you want what they have. You love to spend time with them, because they have such a soothing effect on you.

Once you find the inner peace that they have found, you can expect to affect others in the same way. Your words by themselves may have little power to influence a person who is troubled. But if he or she senses tranquility and well-being flowing from your inner spirit, that is something tangible and authentic; it is bound to have a calming effect.

The Mind–Body Connection

But the benefits of inner peace are not limited to one's positive influence on others. Another important reality is that people who are at peace with themselves not only have a deep and abiding sense of personal well-being, but also tend to be *physically* healthier than those who frequently experience a great deal of emotional turmoil.

How can this be? By way of explanation, consider the familiar cause-and-effect link between stress and physical response. You are hiking in the woods, deep in thought. Suddenly you almost step on a large snake poised alongside the trail. You instinctively jump backward out of harm's way.

What makes it possible for you to react so quickly? The sight of potential danger triggers a release of adrenaline and other hormones, resulting in increased blood flow, an accelerated heart rate, and a host of other physical changes that prime your body to either fight or flee.

The same sort of physical response can also be triggered by emotions and reactions other than the fear of physical harm. In other words, it doesn't take a car swerving toward you, a misstep on the escalator, or a snarling dog to get your heart pounding and your muscles tensed. Inner turmoil—fueled by anger, resentment, fear, anxiety, or negative thoughts—also brings on a hormonal rush, resulting in such physical responses as headaches, indigestion, insomnia, backaches, muscle spasms, and high blood pressure.

Going further, when inner turmoil is allowed to continue unabated for months or years, the steady outflow of hormones can lead to severe suppression of the body's immune system. This, in turn, creates increased susceptibility to chronic and even life-threatening illnesses of all kinds, from the common cold to ulcers, heart disease, and cancer.

Dr. Carl Simonton and Stephanie Simonton, who have long been pioneering researchers in the field of mind–body communication, sum up this important reality in these words: "There is a clear link between stress and illness, a link so strong that it is possible to predict illness based on the amount of stress in people's lives."

For some time, I had a cursory intellectual understanding of that link. But, more recently, it sunk in at a deeper and far more personal level when, as a ten-year cancer survivor, I began attending meetings of The Wellness Community.

Founded in the early 1980s by Dr. Harold

Benjamin, The Wellness Community is a non-profit support group offering education, group therapy, and peer support to cancer patients and their families. A primary focus is the adverse influence that stress can have on the immune system and, conversely, the positive effects of stress reduction as a tool for treating illness, especially cancer.

The techniques and group interaction of The Wellness Community are not meant to replace medical treatment, but are adjunctive. In participation groups, seminars, and lectures, cancer patients are taught how to reduce stress in their lives through directed visualization and other techniques. They also learn how to regain control over their lives—control they feel they've lost to their illness. Week after week, I met dozens of cancer patients who had found new hope, who had begun to play an active role in their own recoveries, and who were leading purposeful lives.

In my own case, I learned how to create and apply guided imagery to reduce stress and overcome inner disquiet. I came to see, as never before, the importance of expressing rather than suppressing my emotions. And I discovered that love is one of the most potent immune-system enhancers; I realized that the more love and peace I have in my life, the better I feel and the more likely I am to remain well.

Willing to Change, Ready to Act

Like so many people, you are probably sick and tired of the turmoil in your life; it taints just about everything you do. You know how it makes you feel much of the time—tense and explosive. You know how it makes you act, even toward those you love—irritable and impatient. You know how it affects your work, depleting and distracting you. And you also know, beyond any doubt, that the turmoil in and around you frequently sours moments and days that could otherwise be sweet and pleasurable.

In addition, as more and more evidence piles up regarding the harmful effects of stress on your physical self, it's likely that you are more motivated than ever to move from turmoil to tranquility. If this is the case, you have already taken the all-important first step: You've become willing to change.

On a day-to-day, hour-by-hour basis, how exactly does one move from willingness into action? It begins with recognizing and owning up to attitudes, reactions, and behavior that are the cause of so much of our inner disquiet. Let's say, for example, that there's tension in a relationship at home or at work. Instead of automatically blaming someone else for the problem, we need to consider the possibility that the disharmony is

the result of resentment, jealousy, or other character flaws on our part.

Similarly, those of us who are chronic worri-
ers must acknowledge that *we* torment *ourselves*
—and that we worry as intensely about a faulty
toaster, or birds in our fruit tree, as we do about
life-threatening health problems.

Moving from willingness into action also
means becoming open-minded enough to set
aside old ideas and embrace new ones. For
years, I thrived on a steady diet of high drama in
order to feed my need for self-importance. If
there wasn't an existing crisis, I would quickly
set about creating one. Needless to say, that type
of behavior had to go if I was to find even a
modicum of inner peace.

As I gradually became more teachable, I realized that all the self-destructive habits I had
developed were actions performed time and
time again—not just physically, but mentally as
well—until they became second nature. All my
fear, worry, and anger were conditioned re-
flexes. In order to change and begin to live
peacefully, I had to accept and repeatedly perform new, life-affirming attitudes and actions
that in time would replace my old ways.

Inner Peace Is Within Your Grasp

You can find serenity. No matter who you are, where you are, or where you have come from, you deserve the inner and outer harmony that brings joy and purposefulness to life. It's important to acknowledge, however, that this state of mind and being won't come to you out of the blue, nor will it remain with you automatically and forever. Inner peace will come as the direct result of the way you live your life—the values you honor, the choices you make, and the actions you take.

In the chapters that follow, these principles for living will be outlined and explored. In practical, real-life terms, you'll be shown how to use them. This is a guidebook, designed to help you learn about, choose, and apply the tools that are right for you.

We might all prefer a one-two-three formula for attaining inner peace, such as "First you do this, then you do that, and you'll live peacefully forever after." But, of course, that's not the way it works. Each of us has to discover the special combination of tools that perfectly fits our own unique needs.

In any case, if you're truly willing to change and take actions to do so, in a relatively short time—a month, or even less—you'll likely see a substantial difference in the way you experience life.

It's important to remember that acquiring ever-deeper inner peace is a lifelong process. Because you are continually evolving and changing, and because you are human, there are bound to be times when tranquility eludes you. When you lose your peaceful center, you will know where to go and what to do to recapture and replenish it.

2

Altered Attitudes

For most of us, life is lived from the outside in. It is shaped and flavored by what happens to us or around us, rather than by what takes place within us. Our state of mind and emotions are usually determined by such influences as the behavior of our children, the actions of our co-workers, the day's work load, stock market fluctuations, even the weather.

Of course, such an approach puts us totally at the mercy of external events, while blinding us to a basic truth: Life is lived best when it is lived from the inside out. Clearly, we're so much better off when our attitude and perspective—the way we choose to look at things and react to them—determine how we experience each moment, each hour, each day.

Attitude is all-important. It is the mother

and father of our emotions, responses, and actions. As much as anything else, our attitude can lead us from inner turmoil to inner peace—or the other way around.

Along these lines, many people see themselves as "victims of circumstance." They constantly blame outside forces—people, places, institutions, events—for their chronic anxiety and unhappiness. They complain, "She got me really upset," or "He made me furious." It's not uncommon to hear people say, "If it weren't for them [parents, the IRS, the court system, *ad infinitum*], my life would be a whole lot more peaceful."

For years and years, I too blamed anyone but myself for the quality of my life. If it hadn't been for my cold and cruel parents, I frequently whined, I wouldn't have become an alcoholic. If it weren't for my ex-wife, I wouldn't have to worry about money. If it weren't for those so-called professionals I relied on, I wouldn't have so many personal problems.

The point is, so long as we continue to put the onus on others for the way we feel inside, we do remain hapless victims of circumstance—not only in our minds, but in the way we actually conduct ourselves day by day.

On the other hand, once we recognize and accept the fact that we alone are responsible for our feelings and reactions—and that much of our inner turmoil is self-inflicted—we begin to have choices.

Remember this: Nobody forces you to feel or act a certain way. You may be limited in your ability to change the outside event—whether it's an employer's unkind remark, or a hit-and-run fender bender—but you have unlimited ability to choose your own attitude and reaction, and thereby determine how you actually experience the occurrence.

It may have been years since you honestly and conscientiously exercised such a choice. Indeed, you may never have been aware that you even had one. Perhaps, from childhood, you reacted reflexively to the external forces in your life. If things were going well on the outside—if you were receiving love, approval, financial rewards—you felt good on the inside. And if things were going badly on the outside—if you were unloved, unappreciated, or financially strapped—you felt resentful, fearful, and agitated.

But this is today, not yesterday, and the choice between inner peace and inner turmoil is altogether in your own hands. Nobody but you can oppress you emotionally. Neither friends, nor institutions, nor relatives, nor jobs, nor bank balances, nor any external stimulus whatever can sentence you to anxiety or despair once you have learned to make choices.

REMEMBER

· You victimize yourself when you blame others for the way you feel.

· Nobody forces you to feel or act a certain way. You alone are responsible for your feelings and reactions.

· You can choose your own attitude and reaction; you can choose between inner turmoil and inner peace.

Choose the Attitude, Shape the Day

When we wake up each morning, every one of us has the opportunity to make the most important choice of the day: we can choose the attitude that we will carry with us through the hours ahead. And that attitude, as much as anything else, will determine how we experience those hours.

If you awaken with feelings of dread, for example, and choose to do nothing to change those feelings, you most certainly will bring a *dread*ful attitude into every situation and circumstance. Typically, before you even open your eyes, you convince yourself that the day ahead will be disastrous. Within seconds, you have butterflies in your stomach. By the time you leave the house your mind is racing and you're a nervous wreck. When a neighbor or co-worker says "Good morning," it's all you can do to keep from snapping, "What's *good* about it!" And it goes downhill from there.

Or, you could wake up with an emotional hangover. Perhaps you did something really foolish yesterday and can't get it out of your mind. You think, over and over: "If only there were some way to relive the event, to undo the mistake, to change the outcome."

Since that's an impossibility, what are your choices? You can torment yourself with guilt and regrets throughout the day—or you can try to forget about yesterday and take steps to renew yourself mentally, emotionally, and spiritually. If you choose to shape a positive attitude upon awakening—one of lightheartedness and enthusiasm—more than likely you'll have a great day.

I used to believe that my mood for the day, and the attitudes that went along with it, was completely a matter of chance—the luck of the draw. I've since realized that I can deal my own cards, so to speak. Not only have I learned to set an emotional tone for the day, but I've also developed the ability to change a negative attitude into a positive one.

Specifically, I don't get out of bed right away when I wake up in the morning. I lie quietly for a few moments and try to shape a frame of mind. If I've awakened with feelings of anger or fear, I tell myself that I'm not wedded to those emotions and, furthermore, I acknowledge that they have no basis in reality. I then try to focus on positive thoughts and feelings—in particular, the good in my life, and gratitude for the blessings I've been given.

As I go over my plans for the day, I remind myself that I won't be alone. God will be at my side to show me the way. With His help, I'll be fully capable of handling whatever comes along.*

Let's say that you make similar choices. You start the day with a positive attitude, and as a result your experiences are for the most part satisfying. It's possible, though, somewhere along the way, that you'll be caught off guard. Unexpected pressures and events may threaten and even shatter your peace of mind.

It won't necessarily be a single, major calamity that pushes you to the edge. More than likely it will be the cumulative impact of many relatively minor attitudinal responses on your part. It will be your unbridled annoyance at a noisy neighbor, a stolen morning newspaper, or

---

* Each of us has a highly personal conception of God, and this conception includes gender. For the purposes of simplification and consistency in this book, I have chosen to use the pronouns He, Him, and His in all references to God.

an aggressive panhandler that will bring on a pounding headache, stiff neck, or knotted gut.

But even at that point you have a choice: you can return to the positive realizations and affirmations you had first thing in the morning. In other words, it's never too early or too late to adjust your attitude. You can begin anew at any hour, wherever you are. At work, at home, while traveling, at dawn or at dusk, you can start again.

REMEMBER

· In the morning, before your feet even hit the floor, set a positive attitude for the day ahead.
· If outside pressures or events threaten your peace of mind, you can reaffirm your earlier choice.
· You can readjust your attitude anytime, anyplace.

Anatomy of an Attitude

It's Saturday morning and you've found time to walk along the beach—to enjoy the balmy weather, to get a little exercise, to be alone. You start out in high spirits, in tune with the sights and sounds of nature. You're aware and appreciative of the blue-green clarity of the ocean, the coolness of the sand beneath your feet, the pungent aroma of chaparral on nearby bluffs.

Suddenly you spot a mound of trash left over from someone's picnic: beer bottles, watermelon rinds, fast-food wrappers. Naturally, you are annoyed. But then, in no time at all, that emotion gets out of hand and mushrooms into full-scale anger. You become resentful of the "outsiders" who use "your" beach. As your mood darkens, you conclude that the city has been ruined. Of course, the only thing that has been ruined is your walk.

It can be fascinating to objectively observe your mind's machinations in this way. It can also be extremely useful to analyze its provocative messages to you during the course of a day. By doing so, you can discover what negative beliefs you are holding and see how they shape your attitudes and color your experiences—whether it's a simple weekend walk on the beach or your daily interactions at work.

As you gain awareness of your thoughts—seeing them for what they are, and learning to nullify them if necessary—you become more and more able to control the power of your mind, rather than helplessly allowing it to control you.

When your negative thoughts threaten to

drag you downhill, you can choose to reverse their direction. You can drain their power by immediately occupying your mind with positive reflections. In the case of trash on the beach, for example, you might reflect: "Sure, there are those who still litter, but most people have become environmentally aware."

I find that it's a lot easier to change a negative and destructive attitude when I have some idea of its origins. It has become increasingly evident, over time, that my character defects are a primary influence on my attitudes. When I am jealous, angry, or envious—when I am filled with self—my attitudes invariably reflect these traits. So one of the surest ways to temper my negative attitudes is to work on my character defects.

In addition to that, it's become clear that my attitudes often reflect my perception of reality. When I make a conscientious effort to see and accept things as they truly are, I'm less likely to be troubled by distorted and harmful attitudes.

The bottom line is that most of us have much more control over our attitudes than we might ever have thought possible. Once we begin to understand where an attitude comes from —its origin and anatomy, as well as the harm it causes us—we can begin to do something about it.

Judgmentalism: A Common Attitude with an Uncommon Price

Consider, for example, our tendency to be judgmental. We may not be aware of the extent to which this character flaw has infiltrated our lives—or, more important, how harmful it is to us. Yet many of us regularly squander a great deal of emotional energy in judging others. Day in and day out, we snip and snipe at everything and everyone.

We rarely have anything positive to say about our neighbors, our city, our country, or even our friends. On the road, we think or mutter aloud: "How can anyone drive a piece of junk like that?" At work, we whisper snidely not only about customers—"That one looks like she got caught in a time warp."—but co-workers as well—"Why do I always get stuck working with that fool?"

We may think that we're just "having fun" when we judge others in these ways, or that such an attitude gives us an edge of sophistication and superiority. The reality, however, is that when we focus only on what we perceive as negative, we are bound to pay a heavy price.

What does your judgmental attitude actually do to you? For one thing, it keeps you in a stressful state, sending your body's immune system a steady stream of debilitating messages. For another, it detours you from the path of inner peace and most certainly robs joy from your life.

Nor is that all. When you constantly judge others, you are apt to feel that you yourself are being judged in the same ways. You create a mental world where, if you want acceptance and respect, you'd better look and act a certain way. As a result, you are constantly concerned about how others think of you; you become self-conscious and self-critical.

Judgmentalism took its toll on me in all of these ways. Looking back, I can see that it frequently expressed itself in the form of know-it-all cynicism—a sneeringly pessimistic attitude toward just about everything.

Not surprisingly, my cynical outlook contributed greatly to my inner disquiet. It kept me isolated and alone, opinionated and close-minded, angry and afraid.

You can't reverse a lifelong pattern of judgmentalism and the negative attitudes it fosters within just a few days or weeks. But you can gradually retrain your mind to be more tolerant and less cynical; to notice and appreciate the goodness rather than the faults in others; to focus on the positive instead of the negative.

You can begin the retraining process by being vigilant. Be as aware as you can of your mind's messages to you. Whenever you realize

that you are having judgmental or other negative thoughts, stop those thoughts in their tracks
and consciously replace them. While the process
will take time and discipline, you'll begin to
make peace with yourself and the world around
you almost immediately.

REMEMBER

· When you have a judgmental attitude
toward someone else, you do harm to yourself.
· Judgmentalism leads to close-mindedness, anger, fear, and alienation. It adds
stress and takes away joy from your life.
· When you constantly judge others, you
may feel that you are being judged in the
same ways. This will lead to self-consciousness and insecurity.

Filter out the Negativity

Even after you have become convinced that
your attitudes determine the way you experience the world—and even after you've started
making attitude choices that bring about greater
inner peace—it is sometimes difficult not to be

influenced by negativity flowing toward you from outside forces.

On certain days, from morning to night, it appears that all the news is bad. Radio and television newscasters deliver a steady stream of doom and gloom. The paper is loaded with articles about corruption, personal tragedy, and natural disaster. In restaurants and malls, on buses and subways, overheard conversations center around health problems, hard luck, and disappointments. At work, the tension fairly crackles; just about everyone has something to complain about.

It may seem, on such days, that we can't help being swept along by the tide of negativity. So we submit, and by nightfall we're depressed, irritable, and emotionally exhausted.

Yet here again we have more choices than we might realize. We can consciously choose how much negativity we're willing to absorb. We can consciously choose the degree to which we're willing to participate in the expressions of discontent. And finally, we can consciously choose to offset the negative energy coming our way by sending forth positive energy of our own.

We can take this same approach in our one-on-one relationships, when the negativity of a friend or loved one threatens our serenity. We all know from experience how easy it is to be dragged down or swept along by a partner's rotten mood or cynical outlook—to become upset because they are upset, to become disdainful and hostile because that's the way they are feeling and behaving.

As mentioned earlier in this chapter, no one can actually force a negative attitude on anyone else. Several years ago, this truth was driven home to me once again through the assertive actions of a close friend.

We frequently went to the movies together. Over a period of time I had developed the habit of getting annoyed and agitated when people in the theater became noisy during the movie. I would grumble repeatedly to my companion that I was being distracted—that the noise was rude and unfair. Eventually, if the noise persisted, I would shout at the offenders.

One evening, following such an outburst, my friend set me straight. "I love going to the movies with you," she said. "But your preoccupation with other people's behavior is getting to be a problem. Frankly, the noise doesn't bother me the way it bothers you—I tune it out. What does bother me," she added emphatically, "is the way *you* carry on. That's what's really disturbing."

My friend's message was clear, and of course, she was right. Thinking about it later, I realized that she had made a conscious, active choice. She could have passively chosen to absorb and even participate in my attitude and actions, and in the process become just as upset as me. Instead, she chose to ignore my behavior, remain engrossed in the movie, and along with that, try to help me see and change what I was doing. Because of the positive choice she made, she ended up helping both of us.

Transform Your Attitude, Transform Your World

Each time you gain serenity by changing an attitude, it's a significant accomplishment. And the more often you put your power of choice to work in this way, the easier it gets. You come to realize that an attitude change doesn't have to be an exercise in white-knuckle willpower or, indeed, a struggle of any kind. There are many simple yet highly effective tools and techniques to help change attitudes. Here are some of them:

1. *Put it in perspective.* At one time or another we all revert to the self-centered view that the world revolves around us. We feel that nothing is more important than our trials and tribulations, our wants and needs. As we well know, such a distorted perspective keeps us in constant conflict.

We can quickly regain our perspective and

see everything right size—especially ourselves—
by thinking about the vastness of the universe;
by thinking about the billions of other people in
the world, each leading a life as unique and important as our own; by thinking about the gran-
deur of God's larger plan.

A friend once told me about an experience
along these lines that had a dramatic and lasting
impact on her life. Newly sober and, as she put
it, "a self-centered emotional basket case," she
was walking home one night from a recovery
group meeting. The road from the church to her
house led through a wooded canyon, which at
one point suddenly widened.

"It was pitch-black and there wasn't another
soul around," my friend recalled. "I couldn't
stop looking at the sky—it was just blazing with
stars. I watched the blinking lights of four or five
airplanes moving in different directions. It struck
me that each of those planes carried two hundred or three hundred people, each going somewhere special, each living a different life in a
different place.

"I suddenly had the profound realization
that there's far more to this world than just me
and my recovery," she continued. "It was one of
those things that people had been telling me all
my life, but only at that moment did I finally get
it. I felt absolutely ecstatic—not only because it

was something of a spiritual experience, but also because it took all the pressure off me.

"Whenever I get carried away with myself these days," my friend concluded, "I think back to that night. It helps me to put myself in perspective and to quickly change my attitude."

2. *How important is it?* At times, when we get upset over something in particular—an unexpected car repair bill, a disappointing change in plans, a mistake we've made—our excessive reaction can bleed across an entire day or even several days. We're like a dog with a rawhide bone; we chew it and thrash it without letup.

When we're stuck with such an attitude, we can find a quick release by backing off, even briefly, and asking, "How important is it? Is it really important enough to ruin the day?" If we can do that, we don't even have to come up with an answer. The question *is* the answer.

3. *Resetting an attitude.* There are days when we start out with a positive, optimistic outlook and then, for a specific reason or no apparent reason at all, our attitude changes for the worse. We may become nervous and irritable; we may begin to feel depressed and sorry for ourselves.

When that happens, we can choose to take any number of actions—singly or in combination —to change our focus. Sometimes all it takes is a phone call to an understanding friend; some-times an exercise session can completely alter an attitude.

Many people meditate to become centered again. We can read or listen to an inspirational message, or simply repeat a soothing mantra. One of my favorites is "The power of God is within me, the grace of God surrounds me."

4. *An attitude of gratitude.* One of the quickest and most effective ways to alter an attitude is to take a moment (sometimes all that's needed is a few seconds) to literally count our blessings. This is a tool that can be applied to just about any mind-set that threatens our inner peace.

Let's say, for example, that you're upset be-cause your car needs a transmission repair cost-ing several hundred dollars. You can bemoan your fate over and over to anyone who will lis-ten. Or, to regain perspective, you might think, "Thank God I have a car."

Perhaps a leg injury has sidelined you for the second half of the ski season. You can wal-low in self-pity as your leg heals. Or you can be grateful that you have the skill and resources to ski, and that you will continue to enjoy the sport for years to come.

Maybe you're disappointed with the way things are going at work—the raises aren't com-ing fast enough; you sometimes feel unappreciated; you've had to put in a lot of overtime. You can let your negative attitude turn each day into drudgery. Or you can be thankful that you're working, that you have a job coveted by many people, and that, for the most part, it brings you satisfaction and security.

When you pause to make a mental or written list of all you have to be grateful for, chances are you'll realize immediately that things aren't as bad as they first seemed. If you're upset about something truly minor, becoming grateful will allow you to see the absurd disproportion of your reaction to the event. And even if the problem is a major one—a serious illness, for example—you can always find something in your life that will bring about feelings of gratitude and diminish your sense of inner turmoil.

Whatever the case, your blessings may not necessarily be along material lines, or even tangible. But if you can honestly look at the reality of your life, you are bound to find much to be thankful for.

5. *Out of the problem, into the solution.* We all know how a minor setback can sometimes unleash a chain reaction of negative emotions. For example, a traffic delay causes you to miss a plane. Panic triggers anger; anger mushrooms into self-pity; self-pity explodes into despair.

We've all experienced this pattern; we've

suffered helplessly as our emotions and negative attitudes have run their destructive course. However, there are ways to defuse the sequence before it can do any real damage.

First, we can contact an understanding friend who will help us regain our objectivity. We can turn to our intellect and away from our emotions by listing options that will help us solve the problem. Finally, we can assure ourselves that it's not the end of the world; we've lived through worse situations that ultimately turned out just fine.

6. *The spiritual approach.* When you are determined to change a negative attitude but find it difficult to do so on your own, you can turn your thoughts to God. If one of your primary goals is to grow spiritually, you might ask yourself how your Creator would have you think and act.

In my personal experience, I'm far more likely to maintain a positive attitude—and better able to discard a negative one—when God is on my mind. I know deep down that He will protect and care for me wherever I am, wherever I go, whatever happens. So when I turn to Him, I can't help but be reassured and optimistic.

Your attitudes, as much as anything else, define your experiences, shape your emotional destiny, and determine your level of serenity. Inner peace is not a catch-as-catch-can proposition; there are choices you can make and actions you can take to bring it about. Today is an ideal time to start.

3

Savor the Moment, Seize the Day

When we are effortlessly aware of the present moment—when we are living fully in the now, rather than mentally whirling and writhing in the past or future—that's when we're the most peaceful and fulfilled. At such times we are best able to learn, to grow, and to maximize our enjoyment of each and every pleasurable experience.

Walking along a street or hiking through a canyon, we are at one with our surroundings, absorbing a flow of colors, textures, designs, aromas: an ornate detail on a wrought-iron fence; a long shred of bark fluttering from a eucalyptus tree; the bright, piercing eyes of an octogenarian.

Spending an evening with a friend, our attention is undivided. We listen with our heart as well as our ears, tuning in to body language and tonal nuances—grasping the feelings beyond the words.

Working on a project at home or on the job, our concentration is sharply focused. Our ability to process and retain information is at peak levels; we are efficient and productive.

We all know, from such memorable personal experiences, that life is so much more satisfying and serene when we appreciate the actuality of each unfolding moment. Yet most of the time, unfortunately, we do just the opposite. We let the moment slip by unappreciated and even unobserved, because we are figuratively elsewhere.

Our thoughts and the emotions they evoke shift constantly between the past and the future. We worry and fret about what has happened or what may happen; we concern ourselves with tomorrow's possibilities and dwell on yesterday's glories.

Everybody knows somebody who has filled a cabinet or even an entire den wall with trophies, photos, and other memorabilia of past achievements. It seems, in some cases, that they have created altars where they can go to worship days gone by. They ruminate and reminisce, frequently to the point of misty-eyed anguish. Foolishly and unfairly, they compare the way things were with the way things are. By living in the past and giving less than their all to the present, their days are frequently barren and their emotions are tinged with self-pity.

I once built such an altar. The walls of my office were covered with reprints of articles I had written, souvenirs from publicity tours, and photos of myself with one or another celebrity. I kept scrapbooks of book reviews and letters, and spent hours poring through them. More often than not, when I tried to relive past successes, I ended up depressed and dissatisfied with my present-day life.

Thankfully, the period didn't last very long. When I moved from one house to another, I dismantled my "shrine" and got rid of most of the mementos. I've since discovered that I can learn from past successes and build on them, but that I can't rest on them. More important, I've realized, the good old days are not the salad days of my youth or the "glory" days of my career. Rather, they are *these* days, *this* day, *now*.

REMEMBER

· By living in the now, you can fully appreciate your pleasurable experiences as they occur. And there are other rewards as well.

· Because you are not preoccupied with the past or fearful about the future, you have a greater sense of inner peace and fulfillment.

· You can "be there" for friends and family members, giving them your undivided and undistracted attention.

· You can more easily concentrate, process and retain information, and learn and grow.

"I'll Be Happy When . . ."

Dwelling in the past, whether fondly or fearfully, is but one way of assuring a miserable present and a constant state of inner disquiet. Another way is to focus single-mindedly on an expected or hoped-for future event that, we're convinced, will finally bring us happiness and peace of mind.

We say or think, "I'll be happy when I get married and have a baby . . . when I receive

my inheritance . . . when I retire . . . when
I move into a decent apartment . . . when I
finish this project . . . when I lose fifteen
pounds . . ."

Obviously, there are a number of problems
with this approach. For one thing, the future
event or circumstance may never arrive. For another, if and when it does arrive, chances are we
won't appreciate it fully without the promise of
more to come—another baby, a favorable tax rul-
ing, a place at the beach.

The worse part of this contingency-oriented
approach to life is that we endlessly wait
around, instead of making the effort and taking
the actions that will bring us real satisfaction and
peace of mind in the here and now.

Our happiness and tranquility cannot depend on something expected in the future; if it
does, we're like the proverbial horse chasing a
forever elusive carrot at the end of a stick. As
philosopher Alan Watts once put it, "Since what
we know of the future is made up of purely abstract and logical elements—inferences, guesses,
deductions—it cannot be eaten, felt, smelled,
seen, heard, or otherwise enjoyed. To pursue it is
to pursue a constantly retreating phantom, and
the faster you chase it, the faster it runs ahead.

"This is why," Watts added, "all the affairs
of civilization are rushed, why hardly anyone
enjoys what he has and is forever seeking more

and more. Happiness, then, will consist, not of solid and substantial realities, but of such abstract and superficial things as promises, hopes, and assurances."

Is there a way out? Of course there is. We can work toward accepting where we actually are in our life today. Along with that, we can do our best to focus our attention and energy on the here and now, extracting as much joy, excitement, and fulfillment as possible. However, we shouldn't do this in a grudging way, with the attitude that the reality of our life right now is second best to what has been or what we hope will be.

At this moment, each of us is exactly where we are meant to be—where God and our past actions have led us. The more accepting we are of our life today, the more inner peace we are likely to have.

Giving up Today for Yesterday and Tomorrow

Even if you are not in the habit of dwelling in the distant past or living for some hoped-for future event, there's another kind of "time travel" that can keep you from remaining centered in the present. Some people call it *projection*, whereby you create vivid mental images and speculations—usually negative—of events that have recently occurred or may soon occur.

Projection is almost always a distortion of reality. It is powered by fear and guilt, and invariably causes anxiety. You said the wrong thing to someone yesterday; now you can't stop replaying your thoughtless remark. You have a dental checkup tomorrow; for days you've been dreading the worst.

Although I've made progress in overcoming this sort of disabling projection, by no means have I eliminated it entirely from my life. A recent example: I awakened one morning at three A.M., filled with anxiety about an upcoming trip from Los Angeles to Boston. Although the trip was ten days away, I remained awake for hours, foolishly agonizing over such questions as: How long will it take to drive to the airport? What time should I leave the house in order to beat the traffic? What time will I have to get up in order to shower, shave, have breakfast, and still leave on schedule? I finally managed to get back to sleep, and the next day I was not only visibly exhausted but also secretly embarrassed.

The Vocabulary of Anxiety

If you've tuned in to your own inner dialogue on occasion, you know how fascinating or eerie it can be. The brain frequently chatters away like a computer gone berserk, spitting out lightning-fast fragments of information, judgments, memories, speculations, and desires.

All too often, it takes you to places you don't want to go—somewhere in the past, somewhere in the future, anywhere but the present. And it does so with a very specialized vocabulary.

With phrases like "could have," "should have," "might have," "if only I'd," you mentally rehash mistakes, missed opportunities, disappointments, or wrongs committed against you: "I should have held on to that stock"; "If only I'd kept my mouth shut."

Similarly, with phrases such as "What if," "I ought to," and "I hope," your mind instantly transports you to a fearsome future: "What if it's something serious?" "I hope they don't change their minds."

The real problem is not the fragmentary messages per se, but the fact that each admonishing and cautionary phrase—whether it is past- or future-oriented—instantly shatters your inner peace by jolting you with negative projections or painful recollections.

But you don't always have to go along with your mind on its wild ride. Once you've learned to identify your own personal "vocabulary of anxiety," you can greatly diminish its power to catapult you into the past or future. Each time one of the phrases surfaces, it can become a warning signal that can help you stay anchored in the present moment.

It can also be useful to develop your own "vocabulary of serenity" as a way to counteract your mind's tendency to take you somewhere you don't want to go. For example: "I'm here, now, exactly where I'm supposed to be"; "I'm doing just fine—God's in charge"; "All I have is now—past is history, future is mystery"; "Feelings aren't facts."

REMEMBER

Fearful mental projection into the past or future is a primary cause of anxiety. But you can reprogram your mind to serve rather than savage you.

"Now *Is the Time . . .*"

Hour by hour and minute by minute, most of us are pressured by time. We're constantly preoccupied with it or fighting it in some way. We're forever checking and rechecking our watches and calendars; we're overscheduled and late, or we're rushing to get something done just under the wire.

By our attitude toward time, moreover, we

allow it to impose unnatural expectations and boundaries on us. We fret about each passing hour: "I've been working on this since noon; it shouldn't be taking this long!" We despair about each passing year: "By now I should have been a supervisor."

When we allow time to tyrannize us in these ways, two things happen. First, by mortgaging ourselves to some nonexistent past or future period, we greatly diminish our ability to live in and appreciate the now. Second, by keeping ourselves stirred up and anxious about lack of time, time wasted, or time lost, we not only destroy our inner peace, but also jeopardize our physical and emotional health.

If you can identify with such self-generated pressures, you might consider examining and reshaping your relationship with time. Is it a constant source of stress in your life—a vise that's always tightening? If so, try to replace that concept with one that can make time your ally rather than your enemy. It is, after all, simply a numerical system designed to make our lives more manageable, not more fragmented. In reality, "time the tyrant" doesn't even exist, since it's always *right now*.

The point is, whether or not time causes stress in your life is largely up to you. You're free to choose how you view time and how you use time. You can even choose to disregard time.

* * *

Another time-related destroyer of inner peace is the frenetic personal pace we often set for ourselves. We dash out of the house in the morning before we're fully prepared for the day. We drive too fast, tailgating and lane-switching for no real reason. We get caught up in a rapid succession of mundane activities, without taking even a brief respite to catch our breath. Even on a day off, we rush through one pleasurable activity in order to plunge into a new one.

What happens when we spend hours and days in overdrive? We lose our center, and find ourselves off balance. We veer away from our natural inner rhythms and feel "out of synch." We end up tired and frazzled.

Here again, if you can relate to any of these scenarios, you can start making some new choices. Instead of frantically and furiously "getting things done," you can try to approach your activities in more leisurely and relaxed ways, savoring each moment. If you begin to feel pulled apart by the pace you have set, you can stop and ask yourself, "What's the rush?"

For greater inner calm and outer poise, not to mention more pleasurable experiences overall, you can try to live in the spirit of "Easy does it" —and simply slow down.

Life Is as Complicated as We Make It

Perhaps you're saying at this point, "Well, you'd hurry, too, if you had my responsibilities [my schedule, my work load]" or "You'd hurry, too, if your life was as complicated as mine is."

To be sure, life is becoming more and more complicated, in practically every area. Our relationships and dealings with doctors, lawyers, insurance agents, and the IRS are examples familiar to everyone, and doubtless this pattern of growing complexity will continue into the future. Isn't this a compelling reason to do what we can—in our own smaller, personal realm—to simplify our existence?

When it comes right down to it, for the most part our lives are complicated and harried because of the choices we make. We buy a car that we really can't afford, and as a result face a financial crisis every month for the next five years. Trying to be all things to all people, we overcommit ourselves and suffer through hopelessly overscheduled days.

For years I've been close friends with a young couple who have created a lifestyle rife with endless obligations; they can't seem to escape from an ever-stickier web of complexity. They've chosen to live in the heart of New York City, to buy an apartment beyond their means, to commute by car to their separate full-time jobs, to increase their family from one child to two, and while all of this is going on, to pursue doctorates in their respective fields. I wince whenever either of them describes an especially horrendous week—or even an average day. These people never seem to have a peaceful moment.

If the confusion and complexity of your life is robbing you of inner peace, perhaps it's time to rethink some of the choices that determine the structure and cadence of your days.

For example, you can think about your personal goals, and whether or not they need to be redefined or reestablished. You can think about shifting your life's emphasis from quantity to quality and, in doing so, begin to lighten unnecessary financial burdens. You can avoid taking on too much; you can learn to delegate or eliminate. You can start looking for simple rather than complex solutions to daily living problems. You can simplify your needs overall.

Try to remember, too, that even the smallest actions can have far-reaching consequences. Let's say a friend wants to give you a kitten. It may seem a warmhearted offer that's hard to refuse. However, if you decide to take the kitten, be prepared for such added responsibilities as food and veterinarian costs, coming home each day at a certain time to feed your pet, arranging for its care while you are traveling, and so on.

When you are facing decisions and making new choices, whether large or small, ask yourself the following questions: Does this choice harmonize with my principles and direction? Will it simplify my life—or will it complicate it? Is it necessary? Down the road, how will it affect my physical, emotional, and spiritual well-being? Will it bring me greater inner peace?

In the final analysis, by choosing simplicity you gain more control over your life. So choose to discard clutter and confusion, and move toward greater order, health, and freedom.

Anchoring Yourself in the Here and Now

We all know how rewarding it is when we are anchored in the present. Our lives are fuller, richer, and more serene. We also know that "living in the now" remains one of our most difficult challenges. The concept certainly seems simple enough, yet for one reason or another it's difficult to put into practice. Here are several exercises that can help you stay in the present moment, and bring you back when you wander out of it.

1. *Get into the habit of living fully in the here and now.* Set aside a period of time—an hour, a morning, an entire day—to "practice." Make it a

point to give your complete attention to everything you do, whether it's listening to a friend,
reading, walking, eating, whatever. Be conscious
of your mind; when it wanders, actively bring it
back. The more often and regularly you practice
"being present," the easier it will become.

2. *Once you've made a decision to do something,
commit yourself fully.* Don't start second-guessing
yourself. Let's say that you decide to stay home
from work because you're not feeling well. Try
not to spend your time feeling guilty, wondering
what's going on in your absence, or worrying
about the work piling up. Focus on getting better, period.

3. *Turn your thoughts to God.* Whenever you
have difficulty staying in the now—because of
seeming adversity, or for any reason—you might
reflect about God's will for good in your life, and
the blessings you continue to receive. Your faith
in God can help relieve your anxiety and keep
you anchored in the present moment.

4. *Take brief "centering" breaks throughout
the day.* Stop whatever you are doing and, for a
few moments, sit quietly and experience your
thoughts and feelings from a more tranquil perspective. Rest your body, quiet your mind, calm
your emotions.

5. *Anchor your mind.* If, no matter what you do, you can't stop projecting—if your mind is exploding kaleidoscopically with negative and fearful images—direct your thoughts to the sound, depth, and rhythm of your own breathing—to that and nothing more. The idea is to keep your mind occupied—and thereby unable to drag you into the past or future.

6. *Live a day at a time.* One of the simplest and best ways to stay in the now is by living life one day at a time. Resolve to deal only with what is put in front of you today. Remember that each day is a most precious gift from God.

7. *Renew your commitment each morning.* It would be wonderful if you could fervently vow to live in the now and, automatically, do so successfully forever after. Needless to say, real life isn't like that. It can be helpful, though, to begin each day with an affirmation of your desire and willingness to stay in the present—to "be there" completely in order to accept the responsibilities and rewards of each new moment.

Perhaps the most rewarding thing about living in the now is the "living" part, wherein we are one with our experiences. At such times we are sharply aware of our senses as they assimilate what is going on around us. We feel our feelings and are sensitive to our reactions. We are serene.

Think about the last time you were "one" with your experience. It may have occurred while you were scuba diving, playing a musical instrument with a group of other musicians, or playing a highly charged tennis match with a skilled opponent. During that peak experience, nothing else in the world existed; you were undistracted, vitalized, fully alive.

Of course, activities such as scuba diving, tennis, and playing music require a great deal of concentration and demand your full attention. But this doesn't mean that peak experiences have to be limited to athletic, creative, or ultra-pleasurable interludes. You can work toward achieving that same kind of focus and intensity at other times, during all sorts of experiences throughout each day.

No matter what you are doing—no matter what is going on—remember that *right now* is life's essence.

4

People, Places, Things: The Paradox of Control

No matter what our history or prospects, each of us has choices concerning our attitudes, perspectives, and reactions—and whether we live in the present moment or in some past or future frame of reference. From that standpoint, as the previous chapters emphasize, we have control over our lives.

But in certain other areas—those involving people, institutions, and events—we lack control and frequently are completely powerless. As a real-life example, you are notified out of the blue that your low-rent apartment will be converted to a costly condominium. Or, despite no previous symptoms or any warning whatsoever, your spouse suddenly becomes seriously ill. Or, as the result of a merger and subsequent corporate re-organization, your job is eliminated.

Our powerlessness over other people's decisions and behavior can also be endlessly painful and frustrating. It's difficult to stand by help-lessly as a family member plunges ahead with a disastrously unwise career, relationship, or investment decision. It's agonizing to watch a beloved friend destroy his life with drugs.

How do most of us usually react when we are faced with such unexpected adversities or unacceptable events? Very often, denial sets in; we refuse to confront the problem or even acknowledge its reality. We rationalize: "They mixed up the biopsy results." "It's just a phase she's going through."

Or else we become furious. Our rage may simmer for days, weeks, months. We may slip into a bog of self-pity, sinking deeper with each woeful thought: "Why me, why always *me* . . . ?"

Eventually, self-will flares, and we feel it's *our responsibility* to provide a solution. We resolve to "make things right" no matter what. We insist on changes and expect them to be made immediately. We become obsessed; we do battle and try to force the issue. We vow to get even. We plead, harangue, badger, threaten.

As we well know from such experiences, the more troubling a problem is, and the more emotionally entangled we become, the harder it is to admit that we are powerless.

What happens to *us* when we stubbornly try to exercise power that was not ours to begin with? What are the emotional and physical consequences of our useless efforts?

First and foremost, we lose whatever outer composure and inner peace we may have had. We literally churn within and have a constant sense of desperation. We become irritable, and take our frustration out on others.

The emotional stress brings on physical problems. Eating and sleeping patterns go awry. Our immune system is compromised; we suffer headaches, stomachaches, colds, musculoskeletal disorders.

Putting Principles into Practice

However, just because we're powerless over a person or circumstance, that doesn't mean we *have to* struggle fruitlessly to the point of emotional exhaustion. *Just because we're powerless over something, that doesn't mean we can't preserve our inner peace while events run their course.*

As with any kind of personal change, a certain amount of *un*learning and *re*learning is necessary. We have to give up our need to be in control, and then apply the principles of powerlessness and acceptance. In practical terms, this means doing everything we can to remedy or modify a distressing situation, then accepting our powerlessness, letting it go by turning it over to God, and getting on with our lives.

Certainly life offers each of us countless opportunities to put these principles into practice. As a personal example, several years ago a friend and I were traveling through Spain. Two weeks into our month-long trip—in broad daylight in the bustling heart of Seville—all of our luggage was stolen from the locked trunk of our rental car.

The initial shock was followed by a wave of absolute rage; I felt betrayed and violated. Along with those emotions, I was furious at myself for being such an obvious tourist—for failing to heed warnings about street crime in Seville, for parking in the wrong area, and on and on.

My companion and I became suspicious of everyone around us, including the police. At one point I persuaded myself that they were somehow "in on it" and, in fact, controlled a citywide burglary conspiracy. I was riddled with fear.

I compounded my pain and frustration by dwelling morbidly on the value and significance of items that had been stolen. Over and over, I railed about a favorite leather jacket, six rolls of unprocessed film, a journal, gifts for my family I had bought along the way.

After two days of ranting and raving, I was

a complete wreck. I couldn't eat or sleep, and almost dragged my friend down with me. On the third day, she convinced me that we had done everything possible and that it was time to move on.

That night, as we began the long drive from Seville to Madrid, my choices became clear. I could continue to torment myself and ruin the rest of the trip. Or I could change my attitude by acknowledging and accepting my powerlessness over the situation, by letting it go, and by doing my best to enjoy the remaining two weeks in Spain.

Thankfully, at that point I chose the latter course. Looking back, I can see that I unnecessarily put myself and my friend through what seemed like a lifetime of emotional hell.

REMEMBER

When you are faced with an unacceptable situation over which you have no control, you have two choices:

· You can become enraged and filled with self-pity, and obsessively and futilely try to force a change. In the process you will probably become emotionally and physically sick.

· Or, in the interest of emotional and physical well-being, you can accept your powerlessness, let the problem go by turning it over to God, and get on with your life.

The Illusion of Power

When I think today about that theft in Spain, and about similar calamities that befall all of us, I wonder why we so often "do it the hard way." Why do we insist on putting ourselves through a period of gut-wrenching turmoil before finally coming to terms with our powerlessness?

Perhaps it's because the very notion of powerlessness makes us feel vulnerable, incapable, and inept—or that we've failed in some way.

Perhaps we're reluctant to loosen our grip because we're afraid of the imagined consequences. If we let go, we fear, our "adversaries" will walk all over us; cruel fate will deal us an even more telling blow; or it will appear that we don't care.

Many of us find the concept of powerlessness unpalatable because we've been conditioned to believe that the more power we have, the better off we are. Aren't people in positions of power looked up to and envied? Isn't that why we spend a lot of time trying to gain power over others—not only with "bigger house, sportier car, better job" oneupmanship, but also (sometimes unwittingly) with subtle emotional forays against others, including ridicule, guilt-giving, withholding approval, and the like?

That's certainly how I lived my life for many years. As far back as I can remember, it was important for me to have an edge—any kind of an edge—over my schoolmates, friends, neighbors, and co-workers. During the years that I was a staff writer for various magazines, for example, my hunger for power manifested itself in an obsession with job titles. I always insisted on one that would deem me separate from and superior to my colleagues, even if only in my own mind. To me, "associate editor" implied a great deal more clout than "assistant editor"; "managing editor" sounded even better.

The point is, through artifices of one kind or another, any of us can influence and even manipulate other people on a short-term basis. And that may give us the *illusion* that we have power over them. But on a more fundamental level, we are absolutely powerless over other people's thoughts, emotions, behavior, and destiny.

You can gain greater inner peace by applying the principles of powerlessness, and you can begin by learning to recognize the areas where you truly lack control. Look carefully at all your relationships, at your day-to-day work and leisure patterns, at any and all aspects of your life that are potentially frustrating. Then, whenever you feel anxious and upset, ask yourself: Am I trying to fight, resist, or preserve something over which I have no control?

As you proceed, remember that this is but a first step. To recognize your powerlessness is one thing; to *accept* it is quite another.

REMEMBER

· It can be frightening, at first, to acknowledge your powerlessness; it may make you feel vulnerable. But the truth is, in many fundamental areas, you *are* entirely powerless.

· The next time you feel frustrated or anxious, ask yourself: Am I trying to fight, resist, or preserve something over which I have no control?

Acceptance: A Pathway to Inner Peace

Even after you acknowledge your powerlessness over a person or event and concede that there's nothing more you can do, you face a further choice. You can feel sorry for yourself and brood about life's unfairness; you can deplete your inner spirit with such conclusions as "People stink," "I'll never travel again," "What's the use?" Or, so much more constructively, you can *truly accept your powerlessness* by putting the experience in perspective, learning from it, putting it behind you, and moving forward with the flow of life.

Acceptance is a dynamic spiritual principle that can make a huge difference in all your experiences. Acceptance can bring immediate relief from problems that seem overwhelming, allowing you to disentangle yourself emotionally and to regain your objectivity, flexibility, and open-mindedness. As you learn to live life on life's terms—accepting people, circumstances, and events as they are, rather than as you wish them to be—you will surely move from inner turmoil toward inner tranquility.

For quite some time, I viewed the practice of acceptance as a last-gasp measure. In my mind, it was reserved for emergencies and catastrophes. I couldn't have been more wrong. Acceptance can be practiced by anyone at any time, and by no means need be limited to serious occurrences. To the contrary, it can be applied to great advantage in *any* situation beyond our control, including the relatively minor frustrations and aggravations we all face on a daily basis.

It's certainly easy to become upset when there is a screaming child at the next table in a restaurant, or when you are delayed in a checkout line by someone counting out five dollars in nickels and dimes. Such cumulative irritations can cause a bellyful of anxiety for us, with this added irony: the objects of our anger are almost always unaware of our feelings.

Since we are obviously powerless in such

commonplace situations, it is pointless to get emotionally involved. The way to remain peaceful is to be detached. Peaceful people don't waste time and energy criticizing others.

Needless to say, it's not easy to reverse years of habit—to completely change our feelings and reactions toward inconvenient situations and thoughtless people. It takes time and practice to become neutral and nonjudgmental, but the rewards will be well worth the effort.

But what of more serious matters? How can one "practice" acceptance when facing eviction, bankruptcy, or a grave illness?

Let's say that your physician is concerned about her findings during a routine physical exam. She suspects an abnormality and tells you that further tests, including a biopsy, will be necessary. It's Friday, and the studies can't be performed until Monday. The results won't be in until next Friday.

Certainly you are familiar with the feelings that can overwhelm you during such times of crisis. Rationality is hard to come by; you're fearful and confused. "Acceptance" is the last thing you want to hear about; it's simply too abstract a concept.

Actions That Lead to Acceptance

The truth is, however, that the principle of acceptance can quiet your inner turmoil and help you transcend your difficulties no matter what the circumstances. As helpless as you may feel in most respects, there are always actions you can take to become more accepting.

Getting back to the example of a suspected abnormality during a physical exam, you can seek acceptance by first looking at the reality of the situation without emotional distortion. A primary reality is that the doctor *suspects* an abnormality; a definitive diagnosis has yet to be made.

As a second step, you can try to determine what, if anything, can be done at this early stage to help yourself and those close to you. You might want to educate yourself, at least in a general way, about the suspected illness. You might have a constructive discussion with a loved one. You might prepare a list of questions for your doctor.

While waiting for the tests to be performed and the results to be reported, you can try to follow your normal routine. You can literally put one foot in front of the other—one day at a time, one hour at a time—acting *as if* things will turn out as you hope.

Finally, you can gain the greatest acceptance

and peace of mind by placing the possible health problem in God's hands.

REMEMBER

Acceptance is a dynamic spiritual principle that can bring immediate relief from problems that seem overwhelming. Here are four ways to become more accepting—to disentangle yourself emotionally and become centered again:

1. Look clearly and objectively at the true reality of the situation.
2. Determine what constructive steps, if any, you can take to alter the situation.
3. Follow your normal routine, acting "as if" things will turn out positively.
4. With faith and trust, put the problem in God's hands.

Live and Let Live

In Greek mythology, a fabled giant named Procrustes invited overnight guests to sleep in his iron bed. But there was a catch to his hospitality: he insisted that the visitors fit the bed perfectly. If they were too short, he would stretch them. If they were too long, he would cut off their legs.

As farfetched as this sounds, isn't there a little Procrustes in each of us? Don't we spend a lot of emotional energy trying to alter or "fix" other people in various, albeit less drastic ways?

We frequently expect others to live by our ideals and standards—to conform to our concept of how they should be. Or we take on the responsibility of making them happy, well-adjusted, and emotionally healthy.

The fact is that much of the friction in relationships occurs when we try to exert our will over others—when we try to manage and control them.

From time to time, in varying degrees, most of us take on responsibilities that are not our own. We try to run other people's lives, intent on influencing everything from diet and clothing choices to financial and career decisions. We take sides and get overly involved. We even find or create problems where none exist, in order to offer up criticism and advice. We try to "cure" others of their emotional problems or their chemical and behavioral dependencies.

Usually our motives are positive; we get involved the way we do out of concern and love. And because we care, it's all the more difficult to accept our powerlessness over another person, especially when he or she is hurting in some way.

Nevertheless, the result of our "procrusteanism" is always the same. We're bound to be unsuccessful in our efforts to control or change someone, no matter how noble our intentions. And we're bound to end up in turmoil—frustrated, resentful, and filled with self-pity.

And what about the people we try to manage? For one thing, we show a lack of respect for their rights as individuals. We deprive them of the opportunity to learn from their own choices, decisions, and mistakes. In short, our relationships with those we profess to care for so deeply become unhealthy, unharmonious, and strained.

The point can't be emphasized strongly enough: nobody changes until he or she wants to change, is willing to change, and is ready to take the actions required for change. That's why it's so vital to our serenity to allow others to live their lives while we live ours—to *live and let live*.

You may be wondering, at this point, "How is it possible to do this? How can you emotionally detach yourself from a loved one as he (or she) continues his self-destructive ways? How can you stop worrying? How can you get on with your own life and regain the inner peace you once had?"

You can begin by making a decision to stop focusing obsessively on the other person's trials and tribulations. In so doing, reaffirm the fact, over and over, that you are utterly powerless to change his thinking and actions, or to alleviate his pain.

Focus instead on yourself—on who you are, on what you are doing with your life, on what is right and best for you. At the same time, think about these other realities: When you become emotionally entangled with someone's personal problems, it's hard not to absorb their stress. When you take on that stress, you greatly diminish your ability to be helpful.

Detachment, on the other hand, allows you to stay clear of the other person's emotional whirlpool and to retain your individuality and objectivity. Detachment enables you to be empathetic, compassionate, and supportive, while respecting the right of another to find his or her own way in life.

Imagine, along these lines, that your grown son has developed the elitist and self-centered attitude that "the world owes him a living." He refuses to work, and gets along by manipulatively charming a dwindling circle of friends. Because of his lifestyle, he suffers periodic bouts of depression. And when he gets in a real jam, he expects you to rescue him once again.

Imagine, further, that you worry constantly about your son and that it hurts you deeply to see him think and act as he does. You've finally realized, however, that he'll never become re-sponsible so long as you act as his safety net. Clearly, it's time to let him sink or swim on his own.

You've already made a beginning by ac-cepting your powerlessness over your son. Next, for your own sake as well as his, you can let him know exactly how you feel about the role you've been playing. At the same time, with as much emotional detachment as possible, try to help him see what he's doing to himself, and express your concern.

Following these actions, *release him with love*. What this means, in real-life terms, is not turning a cold shoulder to your own flesh and blood, but continuing to care without the emotional deple-tion that comes from fruitlessly trying to "fix" someone.

If you are successful in detaching yourself and "releasing" your son—or anyone else—you will begin to experience not only inner peace, but also a new dimension of personal freedom. Where before you had been obsessed with trying to change a person you love, you now are free to step aside and release that person to his or her Creator—to let go and let God.

REMEMBER

· No matter how noble your intentions, you are bound to be unsuccessful when you try to manage, control, change, or "fix" someone. You end up frustrated and in turmoil. You also deprive the other person of the opportunity to learn from his or her own choices, decisions, and mistakes.

· By remaining detached from another person's emotional whirlpool, you can retain your objectivity and peace of mind, while offering empathy and support.

Letting Go and Letting God

Just because we're powerless over someone or something and have become willing to step aside, that doesn't mean that the situation will always remain the same. We let go and let God not with a sense of hopelessness and resignation, but with the conviction that somehow, in some way, positive change will take place.

What do we actually "let go"? We let go of the idea that we can force things to change if we try hard enough and long enough. We put down the burden of unrealistic expectations and misplaced responsibility we've been carrying. We let go of frustration, fear, anger, helplessness, anxiety—and all the other feelings that have been tearing us up inside.

When we let go and let God, we don't abandon our responsibilities. Rather, we accept our limitations and release the problem to God, with faith and trust that He will provide the solution. Letting go and letting God is an affirmative act of faith.

5

A Power Greater Than Yourself

When I first heard the phrase "hole in the gut" at a recovery group meeting, the hair on the back of my neck prickled. I knew *exactly* what the speaker meant. The expression perfectly described the inner emptiness I had felt all of my life up to that very moment.

I had tried to fill the void for years and years with possessions and prestige. I sought fulfillment in other people and the outside world, always searching for the special circumstance, relationship, or environment that would provide me with a sense of security and purpose.

But no matter where I looked or how hard I tried, I was unsuccessful. Invariably, I ended up disillusioned and alienated, lacking direction and even a hint of real joy. For the most part, life seemed empty and meaningless.

I didn't know it that night, but I've since come to realize that my malady was spiritual in nature. Providentially, a series of events gradually opened the door to belief in a Power greater than myself. Over time, I discovered that true and lasting inner fulfillment—and the emotional stability and serenity that come with it—can be found in a spiritual way of life.

Some people back away reflexively when they hear the word "spirituality." They confuse it with organized religion, or equate it with TV evangelism. They see it as something other-worldly and abstract.

The truth is, however, that spirituality is not at all abstract. Spirituality lies not in the power to perform miracles, to cure the incurable, or to enlighten the world, but in the faith-filled ability to meet life's challenges and rise above them.

Belief in a Power greater than yourself can bring order and purpose to a world that often seems chaotic and unfair. With God as a constant source of strength and good in your life, you can feel secure in the knowledge that He will guide and care for you, no matter what.

In down-to-earth ways, your relationship with God can provide solutions to daily living problems and also help you make the most of every opportunity. When mounting stresses and strains overwhelm you, you can turn to God for solace. When negative thinking threatens your serenity, faith can keep you centered. When you are unsure and fearful, God can provide the direction and strength you need.

As your trust in God grows, you will have greater self-confidence and poise. You will have an increasingly clear understanding of who you are, what you want, and where you are going. You will be able to discover and explore your inner resources and to take life-enhancing risks. With God as your ally, you will be free to do things that were previously impossible.

Moreover, because of your faith in God's unlimited power, you will find it easier to accept your own powerlessness over people and certain events. When it becomes necessary to "release" a dear friend or loved one, for example, you will be able to do so with the conviction that a loving God will guide, protect, and care for that person in the best way possible.

When tragedy strikes, when life's happenings seem unfair and even cruel, you will find acceptance and peace of mind in the deep-down belief that there is a plan and purpose for everything—that each event and seeming adversity has its place in God's larger order.

You will have a new perspective, born of faith rather than fear. And although you may not always understand why things happen as they do, you will come to believe that it is for the greater good, in accordance with God's will for peace, joy, and harmony in your life. Perhaps best of all, you will never be without a receptive, caring friend.

REMEMBER

· True and lasting inner fulfillment—and the emotional stability and serenity that come with it—can be found in a spiritual way of life.
· Spirituality lies not in the power to perform miracles, to cure the incurable, or to enlighten the world, but in the faith-filled ability to meet life's challenges and rise above them.

Coming to Believe

In setting down these thoughts and suggestions about God, I am well aware that each of us approaches faith from a uniquely personal background and starting point—or point of resistance. There are those who already have a Higher Power in their lives—who know from experience the benefits of belief. And there are those at the opposite end of the spectrum, agnostics and atheists, who doubt or deny the existence of God.

In between are many people who would like to find inner peace through belief in a Power greater than themselves, but are reluctant to make a beginning for a variety of reasons.

Some were force-fed religion when they were children and have shied away ever since. Some became disenchanted with God following a personal tragedy; they blamed Him for their pain and suffering, or felt He hadn't come through when they needed Him most.

Others have difficulty turning to a Higher Power because of the egocentric notion that they are capable of running not only their own lives, but everyone else's as well. Still others feel that they will lose their individuality if they rely on God—or that God is harsh, punishing, and to be feared.

Yet none of these preconceptions—neither disillusionment, fear, nor agnosticism—need stand in your way on the path to inner peace through spirituality. Granted, they are problems to be overcome. But if you approach them with a degree of humility that says, "I may not have all the answers; I am open; I am willing to listen," you will surely succeed.

To make a beginning, try to put aside your old ideas so that you can become receptive to new ones. Open your mind to the *possibility* that an all-powerful and loving God can bring you serenity.

Because I had been raised as an atheist, I vehemently denied that possibility for a great many years. I viewed spiritual leaders as liars, hypocrites, and thieves. I had nothing but contempt for people who believed in God; they were suckers who lived in a dreamworld.

Growing up, and well into adulthood, my credo was self-sufficiency. As I saw it, nothing beyond my own intellect and willpower could be of any possible use to me; I alone was in charge of my life and destiny. Yet in spite of my egocentricity (or more likely *because* of it), I was riddled with fear and constantly in turmoil.

Ironically, as hypercritical as I was of people who were dependent on a holy spirit—God, or whatever—I had become totally dependent on spirits of another kind. The more disillusioned, angry, and alienated I became, the more I drank. And as time went on, the disease of alcoholism drew me ever closer to the gates of insanity and death.

When I finally sought help in a recovery group, I was told that only a Power greater than myself could relieve my obsession to drink and, moreover, help me put my shattered life back together. I became a member of the group because I had nowhere else to turn, but I stubbornly held on to my atheism.

For a few years I was able to stay sober by being around other recovering alcoholics, but eventually I was once again miserable, full of pain, and dangerously close to drinking. It was then adamantly pointed out to me that I could either face an alcoholic death or begin to live my life on a spiritual basis. Needless to say, that was not an easy choice for a lifelong atheist. But in desperation, I opened my mind a crack.

Coming to believe in a Power greater than myself was a gradual process. I had to abandon my deeply rooted old ideas and open myself to new ones. As my faith has grown, so has my sense of inner peace. I have found that when I seek God's guidance, rather than relying solely on my own devices, I am far more likely to be confident, secure, and serene.

REMEMBER

No matter what your background or preconceptions, you can find inner peace through spirituality. All that is needed on your part is the willingness to open your mind to the possibility that a loving God— a Power greater than yourself—can bring you serenity.

A God of Your Own Understanding

If what you have read so far in this chapter interests you—if you are willing to seek a Higher Power, or are at least open-minded—there's no better time than now. As theologian Emmett Fox once wrote, "God is ready the moment you are. There is nothing to wait for except the changing of your own consciousness."

No matter what your background in spirituality, or what your past experiences have been, you can start anew. Even if you have only a glimmer of belief in a Power greater than yourself, that belief will grow as you gradually put your faith into action and apply it to everyday challenges and opportunities.

As you move forward (perhaps tentatively) along your new pathway, remember that you are free to seek a God *of your own understanding.* You don't have to conform to other people's beliefs, or "compete" in any way. There are no boundaries or restrictions to hold you back; you have as much freedom and flexibility as you need.

You may choose to reaffirm or revitalize a relationship with the God of your religious upbringing. Or you may choose to set that aside and develop an entirely new concept of a Power greater than yourself.

Perhaps you were taught to believe that God is judgmental, unforgiving, and punishing. Since you are free to choose a God of your own understanding, why not choose a loving, caring God? After all, that's the whole point. God's love for you is not contingent on whether you please or displease Him, or for that matter on *any* set of standards. He loves you unconditionally, and wants you to be happy, joyous, and free.

In the process of seeking a Higher Power of their own understanding, some people get sidetracked when they try too hard to define God. For example, they belabor and even debate the question of gender: "Is God male, female, or what?" Or, in the early stages of belief, they become confused because they feel compelled to anthropomorphize God and are unable to do so to their satisfaction.

If you have been frustrated in your efforts to define or conceptualize God, remember that it's impossible to "find" Him using tools, such as logic and intellect, that are better suited for material pursuits. Indeed, the more you rack your brain in this way, the more remote and incomprehensible God may seem.

If it's important for you to "see" God in some way, why not look to a force greater than yourself—the ocean, for example, or the universe? Actually, a solid first step is to simply accept His presence on faith alone.

Initially, in my own case, I envisioned the collective consciousness of my recovery group as a Power greater than myself. As time went on, I looked less to outside forces and more toward my own inner spirit. Ultimately, I came to believe that the reality of God is deep within each of us.

That's all well and good, you may say, but how will I know that He's actually present and making a real difference in my life?

Don't get discouraged if God doesn't show Himself in some dramatic way. Don't look for a "burning bush"; it's highly unlikely that you'll witness a miraculous occurrence of any kind. Rather, you will begin to experience God's presence in your own changed feelings and behavior, and in the actions of others. For it is truly said that He works through people.

This point has been well made by author and spiritual guide Henri Nouwen. "Somehow, I keep expecting loud and impressive events to convince me and others of God's saving power," he writes, "but over and over again I am reminded that spectacles, power plays, and big events are the ways of the world."

Nouwen adds: "When I have no eyes for the small signs of God's presence—the smile of a baby, the carefree play of children, the words of encouragement and gestures of love offered by friends—I will always remain tempted to despair."

REMEMBER

· You have as much freedom and flexibility as you need in choosing a God of your own understanding. There are no boundaries or restrictions to hold you back.
· If you have been frustrated in your efforts to define, conceptualize, or experience God using tools such as logic or intellect, try to simply rely on faith alone. Over time, you will begin to experience God's presence in your own changed feelings and behavior, and in the actions of others.

Building a Relationship with God

As you may already have discovered, the closer you are to God, the more peaceful you feel. It follows that you will want to develop an ever-stronger relationship with your Higher Power.

How can you best do this? How is it possible to move closer and closer to a spiritual force that is difficult to visualize and all but impossible to define?

One of the best ways is through prayer and meditation, which brings us not only a real sense of closeness with our Higher Power, but also guidance and strength. It has been said that prayer is the way we talk to God and that meditation is the way we listen to Him.

Through prayer, we reveal the content of our secret heart—our desires and fears, or our gratitude. Prayer is also our way of asking God for knowledge of His will for us, and the power to carry it out. Through meditation, we still our minds and seek direction from God.

When you first try to communicate with your Higher Power, you may feel awkward and unsure of yourself, and even self-conscious. Don't be put off or alarmed by such feelings; they are natural to someone who hasn't prayed before or whose prayers in the past have been impersonal or done by rote.

As with any other worthwhile pursuit, prayer takes practice. If you make the effort to pray *regularly*—and that truly is the key—it will soon become a more natural and fulfilling part of your life.

Perhaps you are reluctant to begin praying because of fear. That feeling, too, is not an uncommon one. To overcome it, try to pinpoint what you are actually afraid of. Low self-esteem could be the problem; you may feel you're not "important enough" for God's attention. Or, more likely, you may be afraid you won't pray "correctly."

Here again, there is no "right" way to pray and meditate, just as there is no "right" concept of God. The way you communicate with your Higher Power is extremely personal, and the choice of format or words is entirely up to you.

In prayer, it is the thought and feeling that matters, not the words. Some people are comfortable with many words, while others find that a few simple phrases work best. All you really need when you pray is an honest and open heart. God already knows what you are trying to convey. He understands you better than you understand yourself.

Each time you turn to God for guidance and courage during periods of adversity, and He comes through, your faith is strengthened. As your relationship with Him deepens, you become more trusting and put ever-greater reliance on Him. However, if you pray only when you have a problem, you will shortchange yourself. By praying regularly, during good times as well as bad, you will broaden and deepen the channel between yourself and God. Your relationship with Him will mature, and your life will be enriched in ways you could not have imagined.

Don't be discouraged if, despite regular prayer and meditation, you sometimes feel distanced from God. This is quite common; most of us go through it periodically. When it happens to me, I try to remember that, in some ways, my relationship with God is not unlike any other relationship—there are ups and downs. When God seems far away, I do my best to be patient, and I act "as if" He is as close as ever. I remind myself that the distance between us—rather, what I *perceive* as the distance—is only temporary, and that a sense of closeness will return as long as I continue to seek Him.

REMEMBER

How you choose to communicate with your
Higher Power is entirely up to you. There is
no "right" way. It is the thought, feeling,
and regularity that matters, not the words
or method.

Gaining Inner Peace Through
Spirituality

As you progress along the spiritual path,
you'll come to see that reliance on God is by no
means a passive act. In other words, you don't
simply become a "believer" and, without effort
on your part, feel good, and peaceful, from then
on. For faith to become a useful part of your life,
it must be practiced and applied.

Specifically, your faith (and growing ability
to communicate with God) is a valuable tool that
can be used to overcome negative attitudes and
any number of unsettling emotions, from impatience and envy to fear and anger.

At any time and in any place, no matter
what is occurring, you can always briefly stop
what you are doing, put your feelings temporarily on hold, and focus your thoughts on God.

If, for example, you suddenly become ill or require a surgical procedure, turn to God for courage and strength to meet the health challenge. Find comfort in knowing that He will care for you and that His healing power is already at work.

If you are anguished over the breakup of a relationship, regain your equilibrium by remembering that God has a long-term plan for your good. From that standpoint, perhaps the relationship was not meant to continue because there are better things in store.

If you feel unsettled and overwhelmed by the changes involved in moving from one residence or city to another, turn to God as a source of stability and serenity. With God at your side, you won't feel alone, and the necessary adjustments will be easier to face.

Perhaps your inner turmoil is "free-floating" and not connected to a particular problem or event. Perhaps it is difficult for you to concentrate or relax. At those times, too, you can quiet your emotions and regain a sense of calm by centering your thoughts on God.

Think about some of the things you've come to know about God: that He loves you deeply and unconditionally; that He will always provide for your needs; that He is omniscient and present everywhere; that He has the power to bring peace and harmony to your life.

6

Surrendering to Win

A close friend of mine had accumulated a nest egg of almost $200,000 during the course of her ten-year acting career. From the beginning, she had invested the savings with a highly recommended firm that specialized in mortgage trust deeds. Month after month, without fail, she received an interest check. As her investment grew over the years, so did her earnings.

Suddenly the checks stopped coming. My friend made numerous frantic phone calls to the company but couldn't get a straight answer. Finally, after weeks of anguished speculation and fruitless inquiries, she was notified that the firm was in financial ruins and had filed for bankruptcy. It quickly became clear that years would pass before she would recoup even a small fraction of her investment.

"Can you imagine how devastated I've been?" she confided to me. "That money was going to take care of my retirement.

"The first couple of months were absolute hell for me," she said. "I was in a state of shock, absolutely petrified with fear. And I was also furious, not only at the company for their incompetence and dishonesty, but also at myself for putting all my eggs into one high-risk basket."

Even though a year had passed, my friend added, she was still in turmoil. Only recently had she begun to recover emotionally from the setback.

Has anything similar ever happened to you? If not specifically, can you relate to the type of incident? Perhaps you were unceremoniously passed over for a long-awaited and well-deserved job promotion. Perhaps the movers irreparably damaged a treasured family heirloom. Or perhaps a speeding motorist killed your beloved pet.

If so, think back to the way you reacted. Did you become enraged and lose control? Did you conclude that most people are "idiots" and "animals"? Did you carry your resentment around for weeks or months, and fume endlessly about the incident to everyone you know? Did you fall apart and "lose" something of yourself?

It's understandable to be very upset in such

situations. However, let's consider other ways of dealing with them. To begin with, once you have gotten through the initial trauma, you can remind yourself that while the incident itself is purely external, the way you experience it—that is, your reaction—is strictly internal, and yours alone.

Next, with all the objectivity you can muster, you can determine what steps, if any, can be taken to change things for the better. After you've done everything possible, you can try to accept your powerlessness.

Finally, and most important, you can practice the principle of surrender, by drawing back from the conflict and putting aside your own will in favor of God's will.

You may be saying at this point, "Here we go again. I'm facing serious and even threatening situations, and I'm being advised to 'let it go and turn it over to God.' How is *that* going to help?"

The practice of surrender as a solution can indeed seem "too spiritual" in a dog-eat-dog world. After all, don't we have to stand up for ourselves and fight for what's ours? Don't we have a right to speak up and even retaliate when we're wronged?

We can do anything we want—if we're willing to pay the price. We can take on people, institutions, and situations. We can fight tooth and nail to get even, to overcome someone, to change the outcome of something. But more often than not it will be at the expense of our own inner peace and physical well-being.

Again, think back to the last time you "did battle"—with a hospital bureaucrat, an insurance company, a supervisor at work, a moving company, a neighbor, your spouse. Try to remember your emotional state afterward. Chances are you felt embarrassed, frustrated, angry, and, ultimately, exhausted. Was it worth the price?

What Is Surrender?

Many of us have been in conflict with the world around us and ourselves for years. We wage war against institutions large and small. We go head-to-head with co-workers, friends, and loved ones, expecting them to live by our ideals and standards, and to do things our way. We battle our own emotions, obsessions, and limitations. As already indicated, however, it is possible to live far more peacefully by practicing the spiritual principle of surrender.

What exactly is surrender, and how does one go about it?

When we've taken every constructive action we can think of to solve a problem and nothing seems to help, we draw back. We stop trying to figure it out, to deal with it, or to overcome it by relying on our own limited resources. We surrender the problem to a Power greater than ourselves, letting go and letting God. We place our lives totally in His hands, trusting that He will bring us through in the best way possible.

By surrendering in this manner, we make a decision to move away from worry and anxiety, and toward harmony and serenity. We're then free to go about our business in a more relaxed and peaceful frame of mind, with the expectation that in due time—*God's* time—our problem will be satisfactorily resolved.

Surrender allows us to develop and maintain a sense of inner peace without depending on things turning out as we desire, and without requiring people to respond as we wish.

Surrender is the way to detach ourselves emotionally from daily chaos. It is the way to feel peaceful within, no matter what is taking place in the world outside.

"Yeah, but . . ."

Let's face it—many people automatically resist the idea of surrendering. They have been culturally indoctrinated to believe that there is something negative and even tragic about giving up. Because they have so often been told that *winning is everything*—that "winners don't quit, and quitters don't win"—the possibility of attaining something (especially inner peace) by surrendering is inconceivable to them. So, no matter how clearly powerless they are, they simply refuse to give up. As a result of their adamantly held ideals, they become battered and bloody time after time.

They fail to see that by allowing God to do for them what they cannot do for themselves, they can indeed become *victorious* through surrender.

There are those, too, who consider surrender an unacceptably passive and even cowardly approach to life's exigencies. They protest, "I'm not a weakling, and I refuse to be a doormat!" In actuality, however, surrender does not imply a lack of courage or self-assurance. To the contrary, it reflects a great deal of confidence in one's self and God. It takes maturity to surrender.

Some people are reluctant to surrender because they don't trust God. They wonder, "How can I be sure that the solution He provides will be the right one—the one that I want?" They have not yet had the opportunity to realize that God has their best interests in mind always—that His long-term plan for their lives is far better than anything they could possibly conceive on their own.

REMEMBER

· Surrender allows you to gain inner peace
without depending on things turning out as
you desire, and without requiring people to
respond as you wish.
· Surrender does not reflect a lack of courage or self-assurance. Rather, it reflects maturity, and a great deal of confidence in
yourself and God.

Putting the Principle into Practice

Once you become willing, and are able to
put aside any lingering cultural or philosophical
reluctance, you will find that surrender can be
applied to a wide range of issues and challenges.
When a serious or tragic problem such as addic-
tion, obsession, or a failing relationship becomes
so overwhelming that you can no longer cope—
when you feel completely trapped and helpless
—surrender will set you free.

You can also surrender life's relatively minor problems, as well as your own recurring
willfulness. By making a daily commitment to
stop fighting everything and everyone, in the interest of lasting serenity, you can use this highly

effective spiritual tool almost without limitation. Let's look at some typical examples.

There you are, gridlocked in traffic and already half an hour late. There you are, down with the flu on the day of your first sales presentation; or accidentally locked out of your apartment; or at the airport with your flight tickets home on the dresser; or nose-to-nose with an irascible and unyielding landlord.

What are you going to do? You can fume and fret until you are dizzy with stress. You can curse yourself, or someone else, for being so stupid. Or you can take a deep breath, acknowledge that it's all beyond your control, and surrender by placing the problem in God's hands.

Like most people, when I am enmeshed in such frustrating situations, surrender is not always my first inclination. All too often I paw the ground, lower my head, and charge willfully at whatever is standing between me and my expectations or desires. After I've taken the inevitable emotional beating, it dawns on me that, once again, I've squandered my energy fruitlessly and suffered needlessly.

At that point, I move in a new direction and take a different kind of action. I draw back from the situation, surrender it to God, and, in time, find that my serenity has been restored.

Following such episodes, when my surrender has come later rather than sooner, I ask my-self what I was waiting for, and why it took me so long. Pride? Self-will? Stubbornness? Perhaps a combination of all three.

Thankfully, however, I don't butt my head against the wall as often as I used to. As my tolerance for pain and frustration decreases, my willingness to surrender increases.

Self-will Versus God's Will

When we are in a state of surrender, when we try to seek and do God's will rather than heedlessly following the dictates of our own, our days are far more peaceful and successful. We are in closer touch with reality, and more trust-ing of our inner voice. Our relationships are har-monious. We are clearheaded and free.

Yet, even after we have come to understand and enjoy these rewards of surrender, there are bound to be days when we slip back into our old ways. We deceive ourselves into believing that we again need to take charge, that we can and should manage our own life and the lives of oth-ers. We begin to steamroll our way through problems and conflicts, rationalizing, "This is too insignificant for God's attention" or "This is too important to turn loose."

The results are predictable. We end up feel-ing distraught, disillusioned, and regretful for our self-centered behavior. We feel distanced from God. If we let it continue, our willfulness can run riot, not only destroying our own inner peace but also hurting other people.

When these old ideas take root again, it can be helpful to remind ourselves of certain spiritual truths:

· Self-sufficiency is fine as far as it goes, but often it doesn't go far enough. We need God's help.

· God's will is not something to be endured, or accepted grudgingly. He is not the source of trouble and suffering.

· The will of God for each of us, now and forever, is something exciting, wondrous, and beautiful. The life He has in store for us goes far beyond anything we could dream up for ourselves.

How Can We Know What God's Will Is?

Over the years, I have been involved with a number of people who want to practice the principle of surrender but fear that the move from self-will to God's will means forsaking their individuality—their intellect, common sense, and willpower.

Such fears are groundless. Nobody is saying

that our willpower and other intellectual attributes are without value and should be dismissed or "discarded." Just the opposite is true. These gifts have even greater positive potential when they are properly used in attunement with God's will.

"All right," my friends have said, "but how can we know, hour by hour and day by day, what God's will *is* for us? How can we really be sure that our will is in attunement with His?"

More than likely the answer will come, over time, in how we react and how we feel. If we try to be accepting of ourselves and others, and of unfolding events—and if most of the time we have a sense of serenity, well-being, and are comfortable with those around us—these are good indications that we are following God's will.

If, on the other hand, we try to control people and situations, if we find ourselves at odds with the urgings and admonitions of our inner voice, and if we feel anxious, impatient, and out of synch, these are good indications that our will is not in accord with God's will.

REMEMBER

The move from self-will to God's will does not mean giving up your individuality—your intellect, common sense, and will-power. In fact, these assets have even greater positive potential when you try to use them in attunement with God's will for you.

Humility and Spiritual Growth

When I first began to grasp the spiritual principle of surrender, and decided to at least try to stop fighting "everything and everyone," I was told that such a departure from my previous ways would take humility on my part. At the time, I bridled at the suggestion; to me, humility had only negative connotations.

I confused humility with *humiliation,* and thought that it came as the result of being abased or vanquished in some way. As I saw it, a person with humility was someone who behaved obsequiously and could be easily manipulated or victimized.

As time passed, I came to realize that humility is an entirely positive quality, and one well worth pursuing in order to surrender and achieve inner peace. Humility enables us to see ourselves as we truly are—our weaknesses as well as our strengths, our liabilities as well as our assets. When we have humility, we see ourselves in proper perspective with others and the world as a whole.

Moreover, humility allows us to accept our personal limitations and concede our powerlessness over people, places, and things. Primarily, it concerns our relationship with God: the recognition that we have only limited power to change ourselves and outside forces, while He has all power to do so.

The transition from willfulness and total self-reliance to humility and reliance on God can hardly be an overnight process. Time as well as effort are necessary to bring it about. This point was beautifully made some years ago by Sri Daya Mata, the president and spiritual head of Self-Realization Fellowship/Yogoda Satsanga Society of India.

"To grow spiritually we must be trying constantly to change ourselves," she said. "Spirituality is not something that can be grafted onto us from without—a 'halo' we can fashion and put on our heads. It comes from a continual, day-by-day, patient endeavor and a relaxed sense of surrender to the Divine.

"It isn't that suddenly the light of God descends on us and makes us instant saints," Daya Mata added. "No; it is a daily effort to change ourselves and to surrender heart, mind, and soul to God, in meditation and in activity."

At first the daily effort that Daya Mata describes—and the introspection and discipline it requires—may seem awkward and difficult to you. But as you begin to reap the rewards, gaining inner peace and outer harmony, the process will become more natural. At a certain point in your personal and spiritual growth, your new ways of thinking and acting will become almost automatic.

Some people call this transformation a spiritual awakening, wherein they have undergone far-reaching and sometimes dramatic personality and behavioral changes. With God's help, they have found relief from their troubling obsessions, dependencies, and combativeness. They have been able to release their fears and resentments, and to become more understanding, forgiving, and loving.

By admitting their powerlessness and surrendering, they have allowed the power of God to enter their lives and bring about change.

7

Faith-filled and Fear-less

You've just boarded the ancient eight-pas-
senger airplane that will take you from one end
of Puerto Rico to the other. It's the first time
you've flown in a small plane, and this side trip
adds a further dimension of adventure to your
vacation. As the plane rattles down the runway,
you nod a friendly greeting to the grizzled old
farmer sitting next to you.

Five minutes into the flight, a storm erupts
over the mountains. The tiny plane is tossed
about by fierce winds. Lightning crackles almost
continuously. Your heart races, and you hang on
to the armrests for dear life. Your forehead is
clammy with sweat.

As the turbulence continues, the plane suddenly drops several hundred feet. You try to
shout a question at the farmer, but your mouth

is like cotton. At that moment, he lowers his head and makes the sign of the cross, which terrifies you even more. . . .

These are some of the ways we react when we face danger or feel threatened: Our heart rate speeds up and our blood pressure rises. Our muscles tense and we perspire freely. Breathing gets fast and shallow, while digestion slows, causing that familiar "butterfly" feeling.

As we all know, we can react in the very same ways to fears that are less dramatic and less tangible; it doesn't take a hair-raising plane ride to get our adrenaline flowing. Indeed, we can become severely stressed by phantom fears —those that are groundless and have no relation to reality, and those that exist only in our own minds.

One such fear, common to many of us, is fear of people. We're afraid that we won't be accepted and liked, that we'll be hurt or rejected, or that we'll be ridiculed behind our backs. To feel less afraid, we develop various defenses, ranging from isolation to obnoxious behavior designed to frighten off "the enemy." While such tactics temporarily reduce our anxiety and pain, they also shut us off from camaraderie, understanding, and love.

Another fear many of us live with is that of financial insecurity. This particular fear has little to do with our economic status and everything to do with the gnawing, obsessive concern that we won't have enough. And, of course, when we feel this way, enough is *never* enough.

Some people are paralyzed by fear of failure. No matter what they want to accomplish—getting a degree, learning a sport, starting a new relationship—the fear that they won't succeed prevents them from making a start. Or, if they do start, they are filled with anxiety and dread every step of the way.

Still another example of a phantom fear is fear of the unknown. Some of us fearfully wonder, in totally abstract fashion, "What's going to happen to me ten years from now, fifteen years from now . . . ?" Others walk around with a constant sense of impending doom.

Two Faces of Fear

In certain situations, fear is of course a natural and beneficial response. When we face actual danger—be it a lightning storm or a kitchen fire—fear provides us with the decisiveness, quickness, and strength we need to protect ourselves. But, as we have seen, fear can be a troubling and sometimes devouring emotion that threads through the entire fabric of many people's lives.

On the surface, it may not be readily apparent how fear of this kind can influence our decisions, motivate us, and literally shape our existence. But when we think about it, examples may come to mind.

Fear of confrontation keeps us from standing up to a person who continually takes advantage of us. Fear of finding out "what's really wrong" causes us to avoid seeing doctors and dentists, or to repeatedly cancel appointments.

Then, too, there's ego-generated fear, which tells us not to try something new because we might "look bad" and be laughed at.

At a deeper level, some people become "workaholics"—not for personal satisfaction or career advancement, but out of fear of financial insecurity. Similarly, some people stay in failing relationships—not in the hope that they can reconstruct and save them, but because of their fear of being alone.

In my own life, from earliest memory, fear was a constant companion and an unrelenting source of anxiety. My fear of people took the form of agonizing self-consciousness and, even in grade school, turned me into a loner.

Simultaneously, my fear of failure kept me always on edge and dissatisfied. Still another fear—that I would never be "good enough"—burdened me with unrealistic expectations of myself and forced me into all sorts of punishing, self-destructive behavior.

For many years, I tried to blot out my disabling fears with alcohol and other drugs. I sought courage in a bottle but found only a whole new array of fears. When I look back to that period of my life, I shudder, not so much at the fears themselves, or the constant inner turmoil they caused me, but at the way they robbed me of so many of life's joyful and fulfilling experiences.

REMEMBER

Fear is sometimes a beneficial and necessary response. But all too often it can be a disabling and devouring emotion, with the power to negatively influence our decisions, motivate us, and literally shape our existence.

"Afraid? Who, Me?"

As surprising as it sounds, few people have any real idea of how much fear they carry, and of the many ways in which it undermines their freedom and serenity. (I certainly didn't.) We tend to deny that we are afraid, whistling in the dark to delude ourselves, and putting on airs of bravado to delude others. Or we stuff our fears deep down inside, where we don't have to look at them and where we feel they won't hurt us. In so doing, we fail to realize the extent to which fear has made us anxious, has eroded our self-esteem, has ruined our health, or has kept us stuck in an emotional rut.

Clearly, we have to first become aware of our fears—and to acknowledge how they are affecting our lives—before we can undo the damage they cause.

As a primary example, very often we allow fear to masquerade as other, sometimes more palatable emotions. Our fears disguise themselves as jealousy, anger, greed, impatience, envy, close-mindedness, intolerance, or unkindness. However, as diverse as these emotions are, each is essentially a form of *self-centered fear:* fear that we will lose something we have, or fear that we won't get something we want.

In a close relationship, for example, our fear of being rejected or abandoned can cause us to become jealous or possessive of a partner. In the same way, our fear that we don't "measure up" can cause us to become arrogant or unkind toward friends and co-workers.

Moreover, our fear of any number of things —a government agency, a difficult parent, a health problem, an auto mechanic who has us at his mercy—frequently masks itself as anger.

In my own experience, the oppressive fear I mentioned earlier almost always materialized as "more acceptable" character flaws. Although this process took place at an unconscious level, I've come to understand my mind's machinations in this regard. Here's how it operated:

Fear was "unbecoming and unmanly," but it was perfectly all right for me to be *envious* of someone who had what I wanted. It was perfectly all right to be *intolerant* of a person I considered to be "inferior." It was certainly all right to be *impatient* with someone who disagreed with me or challenged me.

As I saw it, *anger* was the most acceptable reaction of all. It cloaked my fear when I felt threatened. And it allowed me to appear manly and tough when in actuality I felt timid and insecure.

It took me quite a long time to become aware of this pattern of self-delusion. Now I'm usually able to get the best of my fear before it gets the best of me. I've found that when I acknowledge and express my fear, this corrosive emotion quickly loses much of its power to harm me.

So when I get angry these days—or when I become aware that other character defects have surfaced—I make it a practice to ask myself, What am I afraid of?

REMEMBER

· If fear is somehow "unacceptable" to you, it may masquerade as other, more palatable emotions.
· It's important to become aware of fear's many disguises, and to acknowledge their negative impact in your life, before you can undo the damage they cause.

Fear of Change

Of all the fears we struggle with, few are more unsettling than the fear of change. We're comfortable with familiar schedules and routines. We like knowing what to expect from our friends and partners, from our jobs, from our own physical selves.

When change takes place, we tend to think only of potentially adverse effects. In far-reaching and farfetched detail, we imagine all the things that *might* happen as the result of a change or disruption. And, initially, we long for things to remain as they were. Here are some typical scenarios.

Your sister-in-law is going through a "midlife crisis" and has to move in with you and your family for an extended period of time. You care about her and want to be supportive, but all you can think about are such possibilities as lack of space, lack of privacy, and your already-tight budget.

Your best friend announces that he is moving out of state. Your first reaction is fear—that your social life will evaporate; that it's going to take forever to find someone as compatible and full of fun; that his absence will leave a gaping hole in your life.

A new manager restructures your job and recommends that computerized procedures be phased in. You lie awake nights, fearing that you won't be able to make the adjustment; that you'll have to work longer and harder than ever before; that someone younger and brighter will force you out of your job.

Because many changes don't make sense, or seem unfair, our initial resistance is understandable. But what happens when fear takes over and we fight change, either mentally and emotionally, or in a concrete way? What happens when we dig in our heels and refuse to accept or adapt to change—when we are unyielding and inflexible?

We feel pressured, anxious, and unhappy. We are at odds with ourselves and the world around us. Serenity seems out of reach.

Human reactions aside, the fact remains that change is the most significant and fundamental reality of the universe. Without change, there is no growth; without growth, life fades. So, despite our fears, we ought to welcome change—as we welcome a spring thaw, a much-needed rainfall, a new life.

Although change is sometimes difficult to understand and accept, we need only look about us—not only at nature itself, but at the day-to-day realities of our own lives—to see that change is usually beneficial.

Several years ago, I was reminded of this truth when my car was stolen. It wasn't an ordinary car that could be easily replaced with a visit to a dealer, but a classic 1970 Mercedes 280SL convertible that I had purchased used, and restored and babied for more than ten years. For weeks after the theft, I was both heartbroken and furious. I grieved for the car, and couldn't imagine ever driving anything else.

But time passed. My attitude changed, and my anger subsided. I received a generous insurance settlement and was able to buy a new car. It still runs perfectly, and it is virtually maintenance-free.

I've grown to appreciate the new car, and I can now admit that the old one was a major source of stress in my life—a bottomless money pit that tyrannized me with its need for constant pampering. The theft was probably a blessing in disguise.

Think back through your own life to one or more changes that you feared and resisted strongly, but that eventually turned out to your benefit. Try to remember, also, the anguish you endured, and the inner turmoil you needlessly caused yourself.

When we are able to accept the fact that everything, including ourselves, is in constant flux, fear diminishes. And when we develop a willingness to flow with change rather than swim against it, life gets a lot easier. Indeed, learning to embrace change is one of the keys to inner peace and a harmonious existence.

REMEMBER

· Without change, there is no growth; without growth, life fades.
· Change is sometimes difficult to understand and accept, but it is usually beneficial. To see that, we need only look at the natural world around us, and the way our own lives have evolved for the better.

Replacing Fear with Faith

It's difficult to overcome fears you've carried around most of your life. Indeed, it can be overwhelming to even think about changing some of the deeply grooved emotional patterns that trigger fearful reactions. But if your goal is inner peace, it's essential to work through old fears and develop approaches that will enable you to deal with new ones.

The single best way to do this is through faith, replacing fear with reliance on God. Simply put, whenever you are fearful, for whatever reason, you can find courage, strength, and solace by reminding yourself that you are not alone—that God is with you, and that you are surrounded by His love and protection.

In a very real way, God can provide the courage you are looking for. It's not that He will miraculously eliminate the danger you face, or that He will somehow erase your feeling of being threatened. Nor will He come up to the plate as a pinch-hitter, so to speak, and take the required actions on your behalf. Rather, He will help you to *see* yourself as courageous and capable, and to *be* so. When you turn to God in faith, He will give you the inner confidence to transcend your fears and again take control of your life.

At times, you may feel that your fears are too insignificant, too monumental, too irrational, or even too silly for God's concern and involvement. But nothing could be further from the

truth. He will see you through any and all difficulties; all you have to do is ask.

Let's say you are afraid to go through with a
divorce, or to apply for a loan, or to confront a
noisy neighbor, or to admit a wrong and make
an apology. When it's time to do what's necessary, bring God along with you. Ask Him to direct your thoughts and actions, and allow Him
to reassure and calm you.

Or perhaps you're facing a major change,
and are apprehensive and anxious about the
possible impact on your life. Here again, fear can
be replaced with faith. Despite the confusion and
uncertainty surrounding you, God will be a constant source of stability and serenity. By turning
to Him, you can regain your equilibrium and
more easily make whatever adjustments are necessary.

When it was first suggested to me that I
could overcome my fears by relying on God, I
vehemently insisted that dependence on anything but one's self was a sign of personal weak-
ness. Since that time, more than two decades
ago, I've become convinced that the exact opposite is true—that faith and trust in a Higher
Power is a sign of courage.

It takes courage for us to admit our powerlessness over people, places, and things. And it
takes courage to place our concerns, will, and

very destiny in God's hands—in the conviction that while we lack power, He has all power.

But faith is more than a sign of courage; it is also our greatest *source* of courage. Faith enables us to tap into a reservoir of strength that is limitless and always close at hand.

Each time we turn to God when we are anxious, confused, or fearful, our faith grows stronger. And as our faith grows, our fears diminish.

REMEMBER

Fear can best be replaced with faith—the faith that God is always with you and will see you through any and all difficulties.

Overcoming the Dictatorship of Fear

Perhaps it's something you've known all along. Or perhaps you've had to learn it the hard way. In either case, the lesson is clear: Unresolved fears destroy inner peace. The longer you deny your fears, or run away from them, the more painful and debilitating they become.

As previously discussed, probably the best way to overcome fear is by replacing it with faith. But there are other effective methods as well. Here are some suggestions:

1. *F.E.A.R. = False Evidence Appearing Real.* Since most fears are groundless or based on negative projections, it's important to look beyond the fear for the facts. When fear strikes, try to step back and disentangle yourself emotionally. Look beyond any confusion, defensiveness, or combativeness the fear may have triggered in you. When you are centered and objective again, you will see things as they really are, no longer distorted or magnified by your fear.

2. *Talk it out.* Fears often fade or disappear when they are brought to light. That's why it's helpful to share your fears with someone you trust. It's quite possible that your confidant has been afraid of the very same things and will have useful insights. In any event, talking about your fears can be a freeing experience.

3. *Is it really as frightening as it seems?* The next time fear overwhelms you, look back through your life and try to recall times when you were absolutely frantic over some crisis. Then ask yourself: "What was the outcome of that big deal? Where is that challenge now?"

4. *Try an altered attitude.* Do you usually look upon a fearful situation as something to be endured, grappled with, or suffered through? Probably so, if you are like most people. Next time, try facing fear with a different attitude. Look at it as an opportunity to learn and grow, a challenge to be met, or even an adventure to be experienced.

5. *Look behind fear's disguises.* When you experience anxiety-producing emotions—such as anger, jealousy, or impatience—try to determine if what you're really experiencing is self-centered fear. Ask yourself, "What's really going on inside of me? What am I afraid of?"

6. *Visualize the outcome.* When fear of the unknown keeps you from moving ahead with a new challenge, or makes you resistant to change, defuse that fear with some advance exploration. Review your doubts and concerns, asking, for example, "What if I try and fail? What if I start out and don't like it? What if I run out of money? What's the worst thing that could happen?" Then, go over each possible consequence and ask yourself, "Can I handle it?"

7. *Walk through the fear.* If your past behavior concerning a particular fear has been to avoid it or run away from it, you can gradually reverse

that pattern—and acquire inner strength—by walking through the fear a day at a time. Certainly, it will be difficult and uncomfortable to do this the first time. Be assured, however, that the challenge will be less formidable the second time, and easier still the time after that. Soon, what once seemed an impossibility will become almost second nature.

8. *Turn again to God.* Any time you are fearful—no matter what the reason—center your thoughts on God. Remind yourself of the previous times He has seen you through.

Getting Rid of Excess Baggage

As a child you were constantly ridiculed and manipulated with guilt. You tried hard to please your parents, but rarely succeeded. So you grew up needy of approval, layered with guilt, and shackled with low self-esteem. . . .

You've been divorced for three years. Your ex-spouse has remarried, but you are still obligated to pay off one of her previous debts. Each month when you write out the check, you boil over with bitterness and resentment. . . .

It's wonderful to be living a sober, respectable life, but you're still haunted by shameful memories and recollections of your past actions. Whenever *something reminds you of the way you used to be-have, you cringe with guilt and embarrassment. . . .*

Even though you are an adult, with your own opinions and aspirations, your life choices frequently contradict your true self. The problem is that you remain enslaved by your family history and are still heavily influenced by your parents' unfulfilled expectations of you. . . .

You consider yourself openhearted and open-minded, and it's relatively easy to share your feelings and fears with close friends. But you've held on to one deep, dark secret. You can't imagine revealing it to anyone, ever. And it keeps gnawing away at you. . . .

Many of us carry around a heavy load of excess baggage—guilt, resentment, remorse—stemming from our past experiences and behavior. Such weighty burdens, and the unresolved issues they represent, are responsible for much of the inner turmoil we so often feel.

These issues usually smolder within us, causing chronic discomfort while hazing our view of present-day realities. Periodically, however, the embers flare into a roaring blaze that all but consumes us. This usually occurs when we are vulnerable in some way—tired, afraid, lonely, pressured—or when a reminder of past pain catches us by surprise and fans the sparks.

So long as we remain burdened with excess baggage—so long as we allow those embers to glow—that's how long we will deny ourselves inner peace. Until we come to terms with the past, it will remain a volatile source of anguish, turmoil, and fear.

We can't change the past and its impact on us by dwelling morbidly in it, by slamming the door on it, or by ignoring it. We can't undo our own actions or change the behavior of others. There are numerous things we *can* do, however, to transform the past from a tyrannizing liability into a life-enhancing asset.

Instead of slogging endlessly through the detritus of years gone by, of plans gone awry, of relationships gone sour, of wrongs committed and endured, we can come to terms with the past once and for all. We can do so by taking specific actions to become rid of our resentments, our guilt, our secrets. We can make joyful new choices for ourselves and find inner peace.

Old Feelings, Old Ideas

Resentment comprises the weightiest portion of most people's excess baggage. More often than not, our most troubling and deeply held resentments were formed during childhood, and

have been kept alive in our continuing relationships with parents and other family members.

Recently, in this connection, a group of
friends and I sat around one evening comparing
notes about our Thanksgiving holiday experiences the week before. We nodded empatheti-
cally as one of the group, a woman in her
mid-thirties, detailed her mother's hurtful behavior and her reactions to it.

"Whenever the family gets together for a
holiday," she began, "I hope and pray that this
time things will be different. But it always ends
up a disaster. I had Thanksgiving at my house
this year, and had planned everything so it
would go smoothly. But my parents showed up
an hour and a half early. I wasn't dressed, the
house wasn't picked up, and the turkey had just
gone into the oven.

"My father went in to watch football and
stayed out of it, as usual, but my mother started
in on me right away. At first she was subtle, but
then she got just plain mean."

We all groaned in painful recognition as the
woman highlighted her mother's verbal onslaught: " 'Nothing's ready. I'm beginning to
think you really didn't want us to come. . . . I
always cover the turkey with foil; it doesn't dry
out that way. . . . This is so typical. You've always left everything to the last minute. . . . If I
knew it was going to be this much trouble for

you, your father and I could have taken you out to eat.'

"At first I gritted my teeth and kept my mouth shut, because I knew it wouldn't do any good to even try to defend myself," the young woman continued. "But as the afternoon wore on and my mother kept attacking me, I finally lost my temper and screamed at her. Then she began to cry, and I had to beg her forgiveness, just like when I was a little girl. It was awful. . . ."

Everyone in the group agreed that the most revealing and painful aspects of such interactions are not the gibes and reactions per se, but the memories, feelings, awarenesses, and frustrations they dredge up.

"It really hits you after everyone has gone home," someone in the group reflected that evening. "That's when you start seething with resentment. You resent all those years of painful experiences and hurt feelings. You resent your own never-ending quest for approval. Most of all, you resent the fact that, one more time, you're overwhelmed with those same old feelings of inadequacy, failure, and guilt."

A Deadly Emotion

If you are like most people, you have had similar experiences. You know exactly what it feels like to be resentful, to carry lingering grudges against people and institutions, to harbor unresolved feelings of hurt, anger, and even hatred. You know that resentment of real or imagined wrongs against you can fester for years.

But you may not realize how damaging, and, yes, deadly, resentments are to your physical, emotional, and spiritual well-being.

To begin with, resentments are a proven cause of ongoing stress and physical illness. This is what happens: Each time you mentally rehash an old hurt, you reexperience the original emotional and physical pain that went along with it. As detailed in an earlier chapter, over a period of time such long-term stress can weaken your body's immune system, bring on stomach ulcers, and lead to chronic muscular tension, among other ills.

Resentments can also keep you raw and vulnerable—in constant emotional jeopardy. In my old life, resentments turned me into a walking time bomb. From one day to the next, my reactions were wholly unpredictable. I never knew when something (and it could be *anything*) would ignite my fuse and cause me to explode.

When you are resentful, it's easy to become obsessed. And when that happens, you are bound to forget your priorities. You may become distanced from God, reverting to your old ideas and old ways.

In addition, when you are filled with resentment it is all but impossible to live peacefully and comfortably in the present. You are simply too busy reliving past events and plotting future revenge. As theologian Henri Nouwen cautions, "You can become attached to your own hate. . . . As long as you look for retaliation, you are riveted to your own past."

REMEMBER

· Resentments cause ongoing stress and physical illness.
· Resentments keep you in constant emotional jeopardy.
· Resentments lead to obsession, and rekindle old ideas and behavior.
· Resentments chain you to the past.

For all of these reasons, it is absolutely essential that we get rid of our resentments, no matter what their origin or focus. Even when we have been grievously wronged, and are certain that our resentment is entirely justified, we still must let it go in the interest of inner peace. After all, why destroy ourselves because of what someone else has done?

Overcoming Resentment

How, then, can we overcome our resentments? What specific steps can we take to become free of this poisonous emotion? Here are some tips and tools that really work.

1. *Take a moment to reflect.* The next time you are consumed with resentment, try to gain enough objectivity to remind yourself of these truths:

· When you resent other people, they are usually completely unaware of it. While you are suffering, they are going on with their lives unaffected.
· One of the worst things about resentment is your endless rehearsal of acts of retribution.
· When you resent someone, he or she lives rent-free in your head. Think about it—your resentment allows another person to literally take charge of your thoughts!

2. *List your resentments.* To become aware of the extent of your resentments, write out a "grudge list" of all the people and institutions who have wronged you over the years. Chances

are you'll be amazed at their number, and at the childishness, pointlessness, and absurdity of so many of them.

In reviewing the list, try to look beyond the wrongs committed against you. Ask yourself: Was I partially to blame? Did my behavior contribute in some way to the incident or misunderstanding?

When you bring your resentments out in the open this way, and look at them objectively and honestly, many of them will simply fade away.

3. *Look within yourself.* When you become obsessed with thoughts of all the ways you have been hurt by someone, try to pause for a moment and consider this: The people and acts that we resent most strongly are often those that remind us of our *own* hurtful traits, capabilities, and past actions. In other words, we tend to resent in others what we dislike in ourselves.

4. *Turn to God for help.* If you are still reluctant to let your resentments go, despite all that you know about their harmful effects, prayer can set you free.

· In your prayers, ask God for the *willingness* to finally release your resentments.
· As difficult as it may be, pray for the person

you resent. Pray that he or she be given health, prosperity, and happiness.

Some years ago, when a spiritual adviser suggested that I pray in this way for a woman I bitterly resented, he told me to try it every day for two weeks. "Even if you don't really want good things for her, and your prayers are just words, do it anyway," he urged. He also advised me to imagine the woman being bathed in a pure white light as I prayed. I went along with the suggestion, in spite of my skepticism. Within a week and a half, my resentment diminished. Following that, as I continued the process, my desire for revenge gradually was replaced with understanding and compassion. To this day, each time I use the technique to overcome a resentment, it works without fail.

· Once you have become truly willing to let go of a resentment, and have cleared the way to the best of your ability, ask God to remove it.

The Healing Power of Forgiveness

By far the most effective way to overcome resentments is to practice the spiritual principle of forgiveness. Forgiveness can free us of bondage to past wrongs, so that we are able to constructively deal with present realities—the feelings of hurt, self-pity, anger, and vengefulness that keep us in turmoil today.

As with certain other spiritual principles, forgiveness is often difficult to put into practice. One reason is that some people have misconceptions about the purpose and dynamics of forgiveness. A common misapprehension, for example, is that if we forgive someone, it will be an admission that the wrong they committed against us was somehow deserved, and thereby justified.

Along the same lines, we may feel that by forgiving, we compromise our dignity and values and "give in" to another person's wrongful behavior.

We may mistakenly believe, moreover, that by withholding forgiveness we maintain an "edge" over those who wronged us. We may feel that so long as we remain resentful and unforgiving, we are somehow punishing our adversaries, and they still "owe us."

Misconceptions aside, the truth is that when we forgive someone, the only thing we give up is our pain. And what we gain is inestimable: Forgiveness extinguishes the embers of resentment that have been smoldering uncomfortably within us for years. Forgiveness allows us to salvage and rebuild relationships that otherwise might be destroyed. Forgiveness furthers our spiritual progress by encouraging us to practice understanding, acceptance, and compassion.

REMEMBER

When we forgive someone, the only thing
we give up is our pain. What we gain is
beyond measure.

To set the stage for forgiveness, try first to
acknowledge that you are entirely capable of
committing a similar wrong or misdeed. It follows that someday you, too, may need to be forgiven.

Going further, strive for understanding; try
to gain insight into the background and character of the person you wish to forgive. Consider
the possibility that the person is suffering as
much as you are and, moreover, that he or she is
emotionally or spiritually off balance in some
way. If you can get that far, ask God to help you
feel empathy.

In the case of my own long-held resentment
against my parents, it was extremely helpful to
finally understand that they had treated me
harshly because of the harshness of their own
upbringings. They couldn't give love and approval because they had not received it themselves. They were abusive because they had been
abused. When it became clear to me that the pattern extended back over generations, I was able

to take a giant step in the direction of forgiveness.

REMEMBER

Forgiveness will come easier if you:

· Recognize that someday you may need to be forgiven for your wrongs.
· Try to gain insight into the personal histories and motivation of those you want to forgive.
· Ask God to help you feel empathy and compassion.

The Baggage of Guilt

"There is no witness so terrible—no accuser so powerful—as conscience which dwells within us."

More than 2,500 years ago, the Greek poet and dramatist Sophocles described with these words the way people torture themselves with guilt. There's no question about it—of all the emotions that keep us chained to the past, none is more corrosive to self-esteem or causes more inner turmoil than guilt. If we are to travel smoothly and successfully toward our goal of inner peace, we must do so without this toxic burden.

None of us are saints. From time to time, we all do things that are reprehensible. It's perfectly natural and appropriate to feel bad about acts of dishonesty, irresponsibility, heartlessness, and unkindness. A problem arises only when we cling to our guilty feelings, do nothing about them, and for months or years allow them to erode our self-esteem and undermine our peace of mind.

I remember all too well the damaging effects of feeling guilty all the time. I was depressed, angry at myself, and always on the defensive. I had a deep sense of emptiness and unworthiness; at any time of day or night, my mind could quickly and easily convince me that I had never done anything right, and probably never would.

I can also see now that I actually got something out of my guilt. It wasn't a conscious awareness, but in retrospect I received certain "payoffs" by hanging on to the emotion.

Guilt allowed me to stay stuck where I was; I didn't have to make necessary changes in my life, I didn't have to take risks, I didn't have to do anything different. My guilt also allowed me to wallow in self-pity. By staying guilty, I was able to please certain people and make them "right," so to speak. The more guilty I became, the better some people liked it.

Needless to say, I couldn't progress in my recovery, or begin to enjoy a new life, until I became willing to let go of my guilt. I was able to do that only when I finally realized that by hanging on to it, I receive no payoffs but only penalties.

Lightening the Load

To identify and eliminate guilt and the psychological harm it may be causing you, look back over your life. Are you still ashamed of past actions? At a certain time, in a certain place, were you dishonest—by omission or commission? Did you cause physical or emotional harm to others? Did you leave someone holding the bag? Is an unpaid debt bothering you? Do you frequently relive painful past occasions when you behaved badly?

If you have answered yes to any of these questions, and are ready to rid yourself of lingering guilt and become free of the past, there are specific actions you can take that will help. Here are several suggestions.

1. *Reveal your wrongs, divulge your secrets.* Bring the past out into the open. Write about the unresolved, guilt-provoking issues that are still causing you pain. Talk about these things with a trusted friend or spiritual adviser. Granted, this

action requires considerable courage, but most people experience a great sense of relief when they unburden themselves in this way.

2. *Make amends for past wrongs.* Write out a list of the individuals and institutions you have wronged and, wherever possible, make direct amends. In some cases this will mean a simple face-to-face apology; in others, you may have to send a letter, or make arrangements for financial recompense.

Don't think of amends as a form of self-punishment, because this will only add to your guilt. Look at your amends, rather, as a freeing and enriching action. Remember that your goal is not to be forgiven, or even patted on the back for your "forthrightness." Your motive for making amends is solely to rid yourself of the guilt of past actions, in order to live more serenely today.

3. *Forgive yourself.* Even if you have thought about self-forgiveness, you may be unconsciously reluctant to follow through. Deep down, you may feel unforgivable—*deserving* of guilt and *undeserving* of companionship, or love, or happiness itself.

If it is possible that this is the problem, here's something to think about: No matter what you have done, God loves you and will forgive you if only you ask. If God can love and forgive you unconditionally, why would you want to withhold forgiveness from yourself?

4. *Live a quality life today.* You can't undo damage already done, nor can you relive relationships and experiences that you missed, mishandled, or messed up. However, you can take the steps already suggested. In addition, you can further alleviate your guilt for past behavior by trying to follow spiritual principles today. In all of your affairs, strive to be honest, tolerant, kind, loving, responsible, and giving.

REMEMBER

To become rid of guilt for your past actions, you can take these actions today:

· Bring the past out into the open.
· Make amends.
· Forgive yourself, and ask for God's forgiveness.
· Make "living amends" by the way you conduct yourself today.

Guilt-givers and Guilt-receivers

On top of the lingering guilt that we feel for wrongful and hurtful things we've actually done, many of us are burdened with guilt that's directed to us by others—parents, spouses, employers, friends, even our own children.

The degree to which we are affected by such "targeted" guilt is usually related to our own level of self-esteem. The less we have, the more vulnerable we are to the gibes, criticisms, innuendos, accusations, and blame-throwing of the guilt-givers in our lives who try to manipulate or control us.

We frequently begin to accumulate this type of guilt as youngsters; we add to it as we're growing up, and we carry the entire punishing burden into adulthood. Some of us, for example, still feel responsible for the breakup of our parents' marriage; for the discord, violence, or drunkenness we lived with as children; or for our parents' financial troubles over the years.

Some of us are still victimized by mothers or fathers who persistently disapprove of the choices we've made as adults; who play the role of martyr and never let us forget the anguish we've caused them; who withhold love, approval, and even validation of our existence because we've deeply disappointed them in some way.

Take the Initiative to Break Free

If guilt imposed by others is shadowing your life and making it virtually impossible to achieve and enjoy inner peace, here are some suggested actions. As you proceed, remember that this sort of guilt has probably built up over many years; so don't expect dramatic relief overnight.

1. *Analyze the emotion and its origin.* Each time you begin to feel guilty—whether the feeling arises from your own thoughts and memories, or someone else's words or actions—try to halt the destructive process with some soul-searching. As objectively as you can, ask yourself questions like these: Is the guilt I'm experiencing based on reality, or is it just an old idea? Did I actually do something wrong? Do I deserve to feel guilty, or is someone trying to push my buttons and manipulate me?

2. *Ground yourself in reality.* As often as you can, focus on who you really are—on your true strengths and capabilities, on what you are doing right in your life. Little by little, as best you can, turn away and pull away from other people's opinions and expectations of you. Refuse to participate in and perpetuate unhealthy family

roles and rituals. Be reminded, over and over, that you need answer only to God and yourself.

Obviously, these are not one-time exercises. They are things you should try to do each and every time guilty feelings torment you. Eventually (sooner rather than later if you are conscientious), you'll become less vulnerable, and more sure of where you stand with yourself and others.

Keep the Decks Clear

While you are coming to terms with the past —taking action to resolve unsettling issues—it's also important to keep a weather eye on your emotions and behavior today. The goal is to live in such a way that you don't allow new excess baggage to accumulate.

As you well know, peace of mind doesn't develop instantly and automatically just because you desire it. It takes discipline and hard work to change long-held beliefs, attitudes, routines, and behavioral patterns.

It may be your habit, for example, to put things off, to gloss over mistakes, or to stuff painful emotions. In the interest of serenity, it's important to deal with these kinds of issues on a daily basis *before* they begin to weigh heavily on you.

Keeping all of this in mind, here are some areas you might want to explore and some changes you may want to make.

1. *Quiet the disturbance within you.* The price you paid for past emotional pain was high enough; you can ill afford any more. So it's essential to deal with negative emotions—especially anger—just as soon as they surface. There is nothing wrong with anger in and of itself; it is an emotion with a purpose. But anger can become a problem when you deny it, repress it, or let it get out of control.

From long and intimate experience, you doubtless are familiar with the destructive power of unbridled anger on body, mind, and spirit. When you erupt with anger, you say and do things that cause harm; you lose perspective and even rationality; you forget about the principles you've been trying to live by. And, of course, if you don't deal with your anger it can mushroom into resentment. With either emotion, no one suffers more than you.

To avoid these consequences, here are some steps you can take:

· When you feel anger rising, take a deep breath, count to ten, leave the room—do *whatever* it takes to delay the eruption. Most of the time, thirty or forty seconds is all you need to decide that you're not willing to pay the price.

· When you become angry, try to look at your feelings honestly and forthrightly. Make sure that your anger is based on reality and is appropriate. Ask yourself, for example: Am I really angry, or is something else going on inside of me?

· Instead of focusing on aggressive action against someone or something, try to approach your anger in constructive ways. Express it when that serves a purpose. Or find another outlet—vigorous physical exercise, for instance—that will let you blow off steam without doing harm to yourself or someone else.

2. *Remain honest and aboveboard.* It may seem at times that an occasional exaggeration, a slight misstatement, or even an outright lie here and there can make things simpler. In reality, however, dishonesty of any kind can only complicate life.

What happens when you are dishonest? You worry about getting caught. If you've lied, you sometimes have to lie again to cover up. Later, you feel guilty, embarrassed, and disappointed with yourself. It all adds up to a bellyful of emotional turmoil. The message is clear: If inner peace is your goal, honesty has to be your way of life.

It's equally important (and, for some people, considerably more difficult) to be *self*-honest. But here again, the rewards far exceed the effort. When you are true to yourself—when you are loyal to your beliefs and values; when you speak and act from a level of integrity that reflects your higher self—you are well along the road to tranquility.

3. *Avoid procrastination; stay current.* Because unfinished business is a major cause of stress, it's vital to take care of responsibilities and to resolve new challenges as soon as they present themselves. That means quickly identifying and handling potential problems before they reach the crisis stage.

These are typical examples: overdue bills that could end up with a collection agency; a dangerous electrical connection that could cause a fire; tension in a relationship that could become seriously divisive.

Keeping your affairs in order can have a calming effect on your day-to-day life. The feeling that your world is "out of control" will gradually disappear. It will be a great relief to end each day knowing that your conscience is clear and that you haven't left anything undone.

4. *When you are wrong, own up to it right away.* Everyone makes mistakes, missteps, and mis-

statements. As part of our humanness, we're all occasionally hurtful to others. It's also human to feel regretful for such errors.

You may be tempted to ignore these things or to pretend they never happened. But even relatively insignificant errors can pile up and infringe on your peace of mind. To avoid a buildup of guilt and anxiety, it's necessary to promptly admit your wrongs, to apologize when necessary, and to do what you can to repair the damage.

Each night before you go to sleep, take a few minutes to review your day. Ask yourself questions like these: Am I holding on to angry feelings? Is there anything I kept to myself that I needed to get off my chest? Was I less than honest to someone, or myself? Did I do anything that requires an apology? Is there something I mishandled that needs to be corrected?

If you discover unresolved issues or unfinished business, commit yourself to taking care of them as soon as possible. As you gradually learn to clear the deck in these ways, you will be better able to keep your priorities straight, to stay on your chosen path, and to maintain an abiding sense of inner peace.

REMEMBER

To prevent new excess baggage from accumulating:

· Deal with negative emotions as soon as they surface.
· Make honesty and self-honesty a way of life.
· Be responsible.
· Promptly admit your wrongs.
· Review your day and resolve to take care of unfinished business.

A Word of Encouragement

At this point, it may seem that the wide array of suggestions and exercises in this chapter are potentially as burdensome as some of the excess baggage you've been carrying around. Indeed, the prospect of doing what it takes to rid yourself of resentments, to become forgiving, to shed guilt, and to keep your house in order may seem overwhelming.

If that is the case, try to remember that you can't discard a lifetime of excess baggage in a week, a month, or even a year—*and you shouldn't expect that of yourself.* All you can do is the best you can do, one day at a time.

However, once you start taking constructive actions, even seemingly small ones, you will feel the difference almost immediately. The hurts you have endured and the shame that has haunted you will lose their power to negatively influence your thoughts, feelings, and actions in the present. By gradually coming to terms with the past, you will gain a new free-spiritedness, and you will begin to know the true meaning of serenity.

9

The Others in Our Lives

There are no shortcuts to self-knowledge and the inner peace that comes with it, but participation in a relationship certainly can speed up the process. Marriage or other close partnerships provide us with countless opportunities to learn about ourselves, to change, and to grow.

Healthy relationships give substance and real meaning to life. They also bring us joy, fulfillment, and a sense of well-being.

Yet, as we all know, relationships can be difficult, sometimes causing great emotional pain and stress. We come together from different backgrounds or generations, with divergent wants and needs. We bring our individual personality traits and excess baggage with us into the relationship. We often have trouble agreeing, compromising, and even communicating. Is it any wonder that successful relationships seem to be the exception rather than the rule?

It goes without saying that harmonious relationships aren't just handed to us. They require time and effort on our part. They also require certain essential ingredients, including the willingness to accept others just as they are; open and honest communications; mutual respect; and active, no-strings-attached love.

Because of one or more bad experiences, some people feel that successful relationships are simply beyond their capability, and that tumultuous and destructive ones are their inevitable lot. That's the way I felt for a long time. For years and years, practically every one of my relationships was deeply flawed. Blind to my own role, I invariably blamed the other party. Only when I began to look within myself for the real source of the problem—and gradually changed my ways of thinking and acting—did my relationships improve.

Unrealistic Expectations

Unfortunately, most of us tend to look not within but outside of ourselves for the components of a successful relationship. We look for the "right" person—with the right background, attitudes, tastes, and aspirations. We say that we're after compatibility, companionship, and closeness. But what we're really looking for is someone who will meet our expectations and fill our needs.

In my own circle of friends, I can think of at least a dozen people who are having serious relationship problems because of their expectations of a partner. One man, still bitter following an acrimonious divorce, expects his new partner to be everything his ex-spouse was not. A young woman all but smothers her boyfriend with demands for attention, because of her unrelenting fear of rejection and abandonment. Another friend, abused as a child, expects her husband to make up for the love and approval that her parents denied her.

What happens when we unrealistically expect another person to bring us the kind of peace and security that can come only from within ourselves? What happens when we don't accept people as they are, but instead see them as fits or misfits of our standards and expectations? What happens when we forget that we're powerless over the behavior and desires of everyone except ourselves? What happens when we try to make people over to match our concept of what they should be?

The relationship founders and fails. We are let down. We are deeply disappointed. We feel betrayed.

The point is, what matters more than anything is what *we* bring to a relationship—how we feel about ourselves, and where we are with our "excess baggage." To achieve harmonious relationships, we must concentrate on strengthening our own inner resources, instead of expecting and waiting for others to fill our empty spaces and "make us right" through their actions.

REMEMBER

"The art of getting along relates only secondarily to the other person . . . The answer is not in finding the right person, but in being the right person."

—Eric Butterworth

What to Expect from Yourself

If your relationships are being negatively affected by your tendency to look without rather than within, here are a few suggested actions. They can be effective not only in existing relationships with family members, friends, and co-workers, but in new ones that develop in the months and years ahead.

1. *Consider others, not just yourself.* When we always insist on having our own way, when we talk incessantly about ourselves, when we are preoccupied with what others can and ought to do for us, people are sure to pull away. There's no question about it—self-centeredness ruins relationships.

It's just as true, however, that relationships improve dramatically when we take steps to overcome our self-centeredness—when we begin to compromise regularly, to listen open-mindedly, to unselfishly consider the feelings of others, and to recognize that people are not in our lives solely to satisfy our needs.

2. *Practice acceptance.* Do your best to allow others the freedom (and it is a precious freedom indeed) to live according to their own personal beliefs and desires—no matter what you think they should do, or what you want from them.

3. *Shift your point of view.* Stop focusing on what you don't like and what you want to see changed in a partner or friend. Instead, concentrate on their positive qualities—on the good, on what you like about them.

Breaking Away from Dependence on Others

When we fall into the habit of expecting other people to satisfy our inner needs, we can easily become dependent on them. In my own past experience, that sort of dependency on others—for approval, security, validation, you name it—stunted my emotional growth and harmed me in many other ways as well.

To begin with, my overreliance on people made it difficult to have healthy and harmonious relationships. Because people were unable to meet my impossible demands, I was constantly disappointed, angry, and depressed. My dependency on others kept me in a fragile and vulnerable condition; over and over again I placed myself on an emotional chopping block.

Each time I relied on someone to fix me in some way—to back up my alibi, to bail me out, or simply to pat me on the head—my self-esteem suffered. And I also paid another, still-heavier price: I lost countless opportunities to responsibly solve my own problems and to find strength and wholeness within myself.

Admittedly, my dependence on others was extreme. But even a limited amount of unhealthy dependence can erode one's self-esteem and cause inner turmoil.

Of course, it's not really possible for one person to become dependent in the way I have described unless the other person allows it. So, just as we must try not to become overly dependent on others, we must avoid permitting or encouraging others to become overly reliant on us. As emphasized in Chapter Four, we only frustrate ourselves when we attempt to "fix" other people or to "make it better" for them in some way—no matter how noble our intentions.

The soundest relationships—the ones with the greatest potential to bring us inner peace—are those based on healthy *interdependence*. Interdependent relationships are built on a foundation of mutual trust and caring. The goals are to harmoniously work out and exchange solutions; to help one another grow emotionally and spiritually; to unreservedly give the best of ourselves to each other without insisting upon or expecting anything in return.

Going further, we can gain the greatest sense of security and confidence by becoming more dependent on God as we gradually become less dependent on other people. When we are afraid, we can turn to God for courage and strength. When we are in need, we can ask God for guidance and support. When we are confused or unsure, we can pray to God for answers. When we feel empty, we can depend on God for fulfillment.

REMEMBER

· Dependent relationships erode self-esteem and peace of mind.
· Interdependence is a healthy and mutu-
ally beneficial alternative.
· True and lasting emotional security
comes from within ourselves and from
God.

The Strain of Competition

Another common problem in relationships
is competitiveness. It expresses itself through
subtle or overt forms of oneupmanship—the
need to always win in games or sports, for example, or to prevail in arguments. Designed to
make one person look good at the expense of
another, competitive behavior also takes the
form of barbs, banter, sarcasm, and innuendo.

Some people get so caught up in this sort of
negative interplay—in the need to be ''better
than''—that it limits their ability to straightforwardly express genuine feelings of love. Without
a doubt, competitiveness in relationships leads
to discord and tension.

In contrast, by respectfully treating your
loved ones and friends as equals—by sharing re-

sponsibility and working together to achieve mutual goals—you can gain satisfaction and serenity from your relationships.

To avoid competitiveness, concern yourself less with what people think of you and how you measure up, and more with wanting the best for your partner, friends, and co-workers—and helping them achieve it.

The next time you find yourself relishing an imagined edge over another person, try to remember that there is nothing praiseworthy about being superior to someone else. It is when you are superior to your previous self that you are truly praiseworthy.

Becoming a Successful Communicator

If you have ever traveled in a foreign country, you know how stressful it can be if you don't speak the language. Communication of even the simplest sort—asking directions, renting a room, ordering a meal—can be an exercise in frustration and anxiety. If you've had the experience, you also have doubtless felt the relief and, yes, elation that comes when you finally are able to connect.

As much as anything else, that's what tension-free personal relationships are about—the ability to connect. When communications are blocked, for whatever reason, the emotional toll can be devastating. Feelings are easily hurt, confusion reigns, and minor misunderstandings escalate into crises. On the other hand, nothing quite matches the sense of well-being and stability you have when communications are honest, clear, and free-flowing.

Granted, it's not easy, even when you *do* speak the same language. Successful communications require, among other things, a willingness to put yourself on the line by sharing your true feelings and opinions; a commitment to being trusting and trust*worthy;* and a great deal of patience.

If your goal is to improve your relationships with better communications, here are some tools and techniques that can help.

1. *Keep the channels open.* Like most of us, you may be inclined at times to keep things to yourself. You may wrongly assume that a friend or partner already knows what is going on inside of you. You may be afraid to open up, or feel that it's too much trouble. You may feel incapable of expressing yourself clearly. You may want to avoid confrontations or disapproval.

It's axiomatic that bottled-up feelings eventually overflow or explode. Unexpressed emotions also give rise to resentments and cause relationships to deteriorate. Remember that other people can't read your mind and are unlikely to "get" your hints. Clearly, then, it's *your* responsibility to communicate your feelings, wants, and desires honestly.

2. *Take the initiative in resolving conflicts.* If you are involved in a dispute or misunderstanding, make the first move toward reconciliation instead of pridefully holding your ground and waiting for the other person to step forward. To open up the lines of communication, usually all you need to say is "Let's talk about it."

Rather than trying to figure out who is right and who is wrong, and to prove that you are blameless, look first at your part in the conflict. Focus on your behavior, attitude, and words, and how they might have contributed to the problem.

If a friend or loved one lashes out at you or picks a fight, do your best to be understanding, compassionate, and, ideally, empathetic. Try to look behind your antagonist's angry words. Perhaps the problem is fatigue, for example, or is health-related. When you are able to "step out" of conflicts in this way, you will likely find that the real problem has nothing to do with you.

3. *Develop listening skills and put them to use.* In communicating with another person, attentive listening is just as important as clarity of expres-

sion. By listening carefully, you show the others in your life that you care about them—that you are sincerely interested in their feelings, experiences, concerns, and joys.

While being attentive is one of the kindest things you can do for another person, it also benefits you in various ways. When you listen, you learn; you feel connected; you are able to become less self-involved, and to temporarily forget about *your* problems, *your* wants, *your* needs.

Think about it: Aren't the friends you value most the ones who really listen to you?

4. *Avoid mixed messages and hidden agendas.* To communicate clearly and straightforwardly, it's important to be self-aware and in touch with your attitudes and emotions. Unless you first "listen to yourself" to determine where you really stand and what you really feel, it's all too easy to muddy up communications with mixed messages and hidden agendas.

Here's a typical example of a person saying one thing but meaning or implying something else. You ask your sister, "Will you need help when the movers arrive?" She replies, "No, I'm sure I can manage by myself." Those may be your sister's words, but her body language and tone of voice transmit something entirely different: she develops a pained expression on her face, and sighs deeply before responding to your question.

5. *Eliminate sarcasm and teasing.* A common but frequently overlooked cause of disharmony in relationships is the use of sarcasm and teasing. You poke fun at someone's athletic ability or taste in clothes. You comment snidely about someone's weight, age, or hairstyle, and then temper your remark by adding, "Just kidding!"

Sarcasm and teasing are rarely as innocent or harmless as they may seem. When you jokingly focus on a person's area of sensitivity, aren't you actually being hurtful? Aren't you putting the other person on the defensive and inviting retaliation and discord?

6. *When criticism is called for.* Giving and accepting criticism is an inevitable part of any ongoing relationship. However, since nobody really likes to be criticized, it can easily lead to bruised feelings and arguments.

When it is important for you to criticize a friend or loved one, first make sure that your motive is constructive, and that you're not being self-righteous or mean-spirited. Try to make your comments in a gentle and even loving way by offering helpful suggestions, rather than by simply criticizing for its own sake.

If you are on the receiving end of criticism,

try to focus on the message rather than the messenger. As you hear the other person out, remind yourself that sometimes the best way to see yourself is through the eyes of another.

Love Is an Active Verb

Many people experience considerable emotional pain and inner turmoil because, as they see it, they are not getting enough love or they are not being loved the way they feel they should be. When they think or talk about love, they do so in terms of *being* loved, rather than being *loving*. And for that reason, perhaps more than any other, they experience an absence of love in their lives.

What such people have not yet realized is that love requires action. As author Diane Dreher has emphasized, "Our frustration comes from defining love as a product, not a process, waiting for fulfillment instead of actively extending ourselves.

"Love requires us to *do* something," Dr. Dreher adds. "To reach out, to act, speak, give of ourselves. In so doing, we become active expressions of love."

To be more specific, on a day-to-day basis we are being loving (and we will *feel* the most love) when we are being kind, tolerant, forgiving, patient, accepting, and empathetic. For example, when we respond with forgiveness to a hurtful act or wrong against us, we are expressing love. When we listen patiently to a friend's self-involved monologue, we are offering love. When we unreservedly accept a friend's unconventional and sometimes outrageous lifestyle, we are being loving.

As you can see, the flow of true love (which is essentially spiritual in nature) is more outward than inward. It is when you are most loving to others that love grows strongest within yourself. Moreover, by putting love into action not just once in a while, but regularly, you can keep it alive, vital, and enduring in all of your relationships.

10

Solitude

"Quality time"—it has become a catch-phrase of our time. We read and hear the words often these days, in newspapers and magazines, on television, and from friends and co-workers. Busy people leading busy lives express concern about not spending enough "quality time" with their partners, spouses, and children. And they recommit themselves to doing just that, by juggling their responsibilities, by rearranging their schedules, by making whatever changes are necessary.

What we don't hear very often, though, are people expressing concern about not spending enough quality time with *themselves*.

Devoting time to one's family, as well as enjoying friendship and fellowship, adds richness to life and is certainly essential to well-being.

However, time spent alone—the solitude that poet Charles Cotton called "the soul's best friend"—is no less vital, and is an important component of inner tranquility.

To begin with, we need to find a balance between social involvement and time spent alone. There are periods when we've had our fill of contact with others, when we've had quite enough of houseguests, parties, and other family and social commitments. So, at the very least, solitude helps us to recover from the emotional and mental demands of such interactions.

But there is far more to it than that. When we're constantly with others, we can lose our sense of self. When we're always surrounded by other people's opinions, values, tastes, wants, and needs, it's hard not to be influenced. The line between who we are and who they are becomes increasingly blurred, and we can find ourselves thinking, saying, and doing things that are truly out of character.

For example, even though we disagree with something, we may give in just to get along. We may be less than honest about our true feelings, because it seems easier that way. At some point, we might compromise our personal standards just to win approval. We may begin to think that "their way" is better, despite our deep-down knowledge that it really isn't. We may even start to doubt ourselves, to feel that there's something wrong with us because we're not more like "them."

Solitude temporarily releases us from such social pressures and influences. It frees us from the need to fit in and get along, and from the temptation to follow the path of least resistance in one way or another. In short, solitude allows us to rediscover and reaffirm our personal thoughts and feelings—the ideas and emotions that define our true and natural selves.

Solitude can be a rich source of inspiration and creativity as well. It provides the opportunity to become more self-aware, and to engage in productive reflection. Solitude gives us the freedom to imagine, to dream, to fantasize, to plan, to rehearse.

A friend of mine, who is also a writer, has spoken to me about the importance of spending time alone. "When I spend too many days in a row with other people," she says, "I lose my creative edge. I'm far more focused, insightful, and, yes, productive after I've been off by myself for a while."

To many people, time alone also is a necessary step in the decision-making process. On their own and away from the distractions and influences of the workaday world, they are able to slow down, to look within, and to calmly sort things out. Instead of impulsively forcing the issue, they give themselves the chance to *discover* the wise and proper choice of what to do or which way to go.

That's what I usually do when I'm faced with a difficult decision. First, I like to discuss the pros and cons with one or two close friends who are familiar with my background and present circumstances. Following that, I set aside time for solitary reflection so that I can listen to my intuitive voice and, I hope, come up with the answer that is right for me.

A certain amount of solitude is also important for those of us who are committed to spiritual growth. We need a time and place where, in solitude, we can gain a feeling of closeness with our Creator. And we need time alone for prayer and meditation, so that we can communicate with God and open ourselves to His guidance.

REMEMBER

Solitude is an important component of inner tranquility, for these reasons:

· It helps us recover from the emotional and mental demands of family and social involvement.
· It allows us to regain our sense of self—to rediscover the values, ideas, and emotions that define who we really are.
· It can be a wellspring of inspiration, creativity, and productivity.
· It can help us make wise and intuitive decisions.
· It can bring us closer to God.

Why Some People Avoid Solitude

For all the advantages of solitude, you may be one of those people who become "itchy and nervous" when they are alone, and who run for cover in a crowd. If so, you can take some comfort in the fact that you are hardly unique; many people feel the same way. If you would like to overcome your reluctance to purposefully spend time by yourself, it could be helpful to look at some of the reasons people avoid solitude.

· Because they were raised in chaotic house-
holds or, for one reason or another, have become
accustomed to constant noise and activity, some
people are put off by the unfamiliarity of solitude. There is something disturbing about the
quiet that comes with it; it feels as if something
is *wrong*. For these people, solitude is empty and
forbidding, rather than full and enriching. Solitude is like a "black hole" that can swallow them
up.

Along these same lines, there are those who
are not only used to turbulence in their world,
but *dependent* on it for various reasons. They frequently turn minor mishaps into major calamities to get a rush of self-importance. They
constantly overschedule their time because they
thrive on crisis. If they are not knee-deep in turmoil, they feel restless and incomplete.

· Some people find it difficult to deal with the
freedom and self-responsibility that comes with
solitude. They don't know what to do with unstructured time, and as a result become quickly
bored when they are alone.

· For people who are lonely, unplanned solitude can intensify that feeling. Of course, there is
a world of difference between being alone and
being lonely.

· In marriages and other close relationships that
lack healthy communications, the need for solitude by one partner can be misunderstood by

the other. For example, one person expresses a desire to have some time alone, for all the right and proper reasons. Conflict develops when the other person, perhaps because of insecurity, interprets it as uninterest, rejection, or even abandonment.

· Most of us like to be around other people, rather than off by ourselves, in various social situations—at the beach, in a theater, and so on. However, some people go to extremes in their need to conform and be part of the crowd. They are afraid that if they spend time by themselves, in solitude, they will be labeled misfits or hermits; they fear that they will be thought of as flawed in some way, and pitied.

· When we are alone, we are temporarily removed from worldly distractions that serve to shield us from our own emotional struggles: guilt, self-doubt, painful memories, resentments, and the like. So solitude can sometimes lead to a frightening confrontation with our inner feelings. Indeed, that's why some of us get "hooked" on noise, chaos, and constant companionship—as ways to block out painful inner realities.

In my own case, even though I was antisocial and considered myself a "loner," I still couldn't bear the self-confrontation that came with solitude. So I surrounded myself with noise whenever possible (a blaring TV at home, a blaring radio in my car), buffered myself with chemicals, or forced myself to spend time in crowded public places.

Getting Comfortable with Yourself

In solitude, you come face-to-face with your inner self. As discussed in the preceding section, solitude can in fact *amplify* your relationship with yourself. If you are not comfortable in that relationship, you will not be comfortable alone. In other words, the more self-acceptance you have, the more peaceful you will be during times of solitude and the more benefits you will gain.

This is not to say that you should forgo time alone if you are not yet comfortable with yourself. As a matter of fact, if you are willing to be patient during your initial experiments with solitude, you will become progressively more insightful and self-aware. And these qualities, in turn, will lead you to greater self-acceptance.

Self-acceptance, in its complete and ideal form, means honoring and loving yourself exactly as you are, at this very moment. It means embracing all of yourself, every bit of yourself, not just the "good stuff." This includes the qualities and characteristics you may not acknowledge as assets—warmheartedness, for example, or teachability. It also includes what you may consider liabilities and would prefer to disown—moodiness and impulsiveness, for example, or above- or below-average height and weight.

What self-acceptance is *not* is a surrender—a reluctant *concession* to the fact that you are the way you are; that you will never again be at the "peak" of your past; or that you will never become what you once hoped to be.

REMEMBER

· Self-acceptance comes from discovering or rediscovering the unique qualities that make you who you are, and then learning to value and even treasure those qualities.
· Self-acceptance is an antidote to painful self-judgment.
· It is perfectly all right to be yourself, even if that means being different from other people.
· It is far easier to become self-accepting than it is to constantly pretend to be something you are not.
· Self-acceptance leads to peaceful solitude, and solitude leads to greater self-acceptance.

Developing a Taste for Solitude

1. *Program the time.* If in the past you have feared or avoided solitude for any reason, and now are ready to see what it can do for you, a good way to begin is by actually scheduling time to be alone. Of course, the amount of time and frequency will depend on your lifestyle, responsibilities, and temperament. To begin with, you may want to set aside as little as twenty minutes a day, or as much as an hour. Later, you may look forward to entire afternoons or entire days by yourself.

2. *Be patient—tranquility is closer than you realize.* Approach your initial period of solitude with an open mind. See what happens. You may develop a taste for it right away, or you may be somewhat uncomfortable at first. If you do feel restless or nervous, try to tough it out for a little while. That way, you can at least find out what's making you uncomfortable and work on that area.

However, if you have begun to follow some of the suggestions in the preceding chapters, it is less likely that you will be uncomfortable. By learning how to alter your attitudes and deal with fear and anger, you have fewer emotional upheavals. By taking actions to come to terms with the past, you are becoming free of guilt, shame, and remorse. By learning to live in the present moment, you are sparing yourself the anxiety of negative projection. So you are probably more at peace than ever before, not only when you are alone, but when you are with others.

3. *Explain why and how.* Before you make periods of solitude a regular part of your routine, have a talk with your partner or spouse. In the interest of full understanding, explain exactly why you will be scheduling time alone. Make it clear that your goal is to become more self-aware, centered, and peaceful. Be sure to emphasize that your time alone has nothing to do with "getting away" from him or her.

4. *This is your time.* Planned solitude is not a time to "get things done" so that they can be crossed off your list. However, that doesn't mean you have to sit motionless, doing nothing, to benefit from solitude. Some people find it very relaxing to leisurely browse through boxes of memorabilia and photos, for example, or to thumb through magazines.

5. *Avoiding boredom.* If you tend to become bored with unstructured time, you might try to set one or more simple and stress-free "goals"

for yourself. It could be along the lines of trying not to take yourself so seriously, or giving yourself permission to be less inhibited and more flexible. You might want to start keeping a journal, jotting down thoughts, feelings, and dreams. Another good way to avoid boredom during periods of solitude is to enjoy long, meandering walks—not for exercise or to get somewhere, but simply to be off by yourself.

11

An Inner Stillness, An Inner Healing

Like many people, I sometimes take certain blessings for granted—good health, a place to live, enough to eat, a car, friends. I doubt, however, that I will ever take for granted the lengthening periods of inner stillness I've come to know.

It's not only that I treasure these times of serenity and am grateful for them, but also that they contrast so sharply with the frenzied and unbalanced way I almost always felt and acted in years past.

I remember all too well the torment I experienced growing up, the terror that accompanied my drinking and drug use, and my never-ending fractiousness at home and at work. Hardly a day passed when I wasn't in trouble in some way or in conflict with someone. Inwardly, I was insecure and resentful; outwardly, I was defiant and explosive.

When the pressure increased beyond endurance, which it frequently did, I tried to relieve it by binging, fighting, squandering money, driving recklessly, or with similar self-destructive actions. Needless to say, such behavior only added fuel to the fire in the form of guilt, embarrassment, and more anxiety.

In truth, I did experience occasional moments of inner calm. However, they resulted not from any action or inaction on my part, but wholly from outside events or circumstances—a startling burst of brilliant fall foliage, for example, or an unexpected emotional or financial windfall.

Today, the serenity that was once a rarity has become an undercurrent of my life. Most of the time it comes from within myself and has little to do with outside forces or eventualities.

What has happened is that I've made fundamental changes in my attitude, outlook, and behavior over the years. I've learned to temper my reactions, to seek out constructive rather than destructive ways to deal with stress, and to apply spiritual solutions to everyday living problems.

I've been taught, for example, how to achieve inner stillness through meditation; how to overcome apprehension and other stressful feelings with mental imagery; and how to become physically and emotionally renewed by applying a variety of relaxation techniques.

Your Personal Pathway to Self-renewal

Of course, your needs and goals, as well as your experience and lifestyle, are personal and unique. That's why you'll want to choose your own avenues of self-renewal. You may decide to rely primarily on meditation to gain inner stillness, for example, or you may be more comfortable combining meditation with other techniques and activities, such as running, gardening, fishing, or yoga.

Whatever forms of self-renewal you experiment with and eventually choose, the whole idea is to withdraw into yourself, to restore your energy and inner spirit, and to bring harmony and stability to your life.

You may protest, "Right now there are more important considerations in my life." You may say, "I can't afford the time, and I don't have the patience."

Be assured that eventually you will feel just the opposite. You'll discover that you can't afford *not* to set the priority, take the time, and develop the patience. Because, by regularly practicing self-renewal techniques, you will become more centered, peaceful, and productive. You will come to know a sense of connectedness—the awe-inspiring feeling that you are at one with your fellows, with God, with the natural world.

You will learn how to temporarily retreat from daily concerns and to recharge yourself, which will enable you to reenter the "real world" refreshed and at peace. You will learn how to establish God-consciousness, and to anchor yourself in faith each day.

Your self-esteem will rise because you are taking actions highly beneficial to yourself. You will grow spiritually, widen your vision of who you are, and expand and enrich every dimension of your life.

REMEMBER

If you think you don't have the time for self-renewal activities, consider these potential benefits:

· Harmony and stability in your life.
· A feeling of connectedness.
· Increased productivity.
· Deepened faith.
· Enhanced self-esteem.
· The ability to function in a sometimes chaotic world with an abiding sense of inner calm.

If you haven't already made self-renewal activities a part of your life, here's a way to get started. For the next several days, monitor and keep a record of how and where you spend your time. In reviewing your daily activities, reconsider any reluctance you may have as to whether you can regularly devote half an hour or so to quiet reflection.

Going further, try to establish and maintain a balance between your career, your family responsibilities, your social life, and the time you take to achieve inner stillness and inner healing. In working toward that balance, remember that you will shortchange yourself—and your world will more likely become chaotic and stressful—if you neglect your spiritual and personal needs.

Learning to Meditate

Meditation is a spiritual practice that people have used throughout the ages to enrich their lives. People meditate to deepen their consciousness of God, to gain awareness of His will for them, and to open themselves to His guidance and inspiration.

People also meditate to find and listen to their intuitive voice, and to gain an inner stillness that will prepare them for the day ahead. Others meditate simply to retreat from worldly concerns, as well as from the outpourings of their own minds.

As part of their quest for inner peace, some people want to try meditation but hold back because of various fears. They fear that awkward and embarrassing feelings might arise; that they are not "spiritually advanced" enough to meditate properly; that God is so remote as to be unreachable; or that they won't be able to quiet their minds long enough even to get started.

If any of these fears have been causing you to postpone or avoid the practice of meditation, it can be reassuring to know that such apprehension is not at all unusual. The important thing to remember is that meditation is an entirely personal and individual process; *it can be whatever you want it to be.*

So you need not concern yourself with whether you will choose the right method and meditate "properly," with whether your motives are exactly right, or with whether each and every meditational experience will bring the results you hope for. All you need to concern yourself with is making a start, and then doing the best you can as the process evolves and adds serenity and spiritual richness to your life.

If you have never meditated before, or have tried briefly and given up in frustration, here are some things you might want to consider in getting started or starting anew.

Give yourself plenty of time and latitude to experiment with different forms of meditation, in order to find the one best suited to your goals, temperament, and lifestyle. Don't be in a rush to "lock in" to a routine that will become an enduring pattern in your life.

Choose a meditational setting that, ideally, will be private, quiet, free of distractions, inspirational, and convenient. Given these criteria, you wouldn't dream of trying to meditate on a noisy factory floor. On the other hand, taking it to the opposite extreme, you need not retreat to a monastery or temple. A lot depends on where and how you live, as well as the time of day you choose to regularly meditate. You might pick a private room in your own home, a patio or backyard, a nearby hilltop or beach, or a quiet corner of a city park.

When you have decided on a place and time and are ready to experiment, bear in mind that there are as many forms of meditation as there are people who meditate. In other words, there is no "correct" way, nor need there be any boundaries. The process can be elaborate and ritualistic, or simple and unstructured. Again, it's entirely up to you. Here are some methods to consider:

1. Anchor your mind by silently repeating a mantra—a word or phrase that has special meaning to you. For instance, use the words "I am" when you breathe out, and "at peace" when you breathe in. You can divide any number of calming phrases in the same way. Two other examples are "Let go, let God" and "The past is gone, this is now."

2. Sit quietly and try to completely empty your mind. One good way to accomplish this is by perceiving yourself as an empty vessel.

3. Focus on the spiritual force in your life, on the Higher Power of your understanding.

Imagine yourself becoming open and fully receptive to God's guidance.

4. Practice meditation in motion. Choose a physical activity—such as running, walking, or swimming—that will keep you fully engaged. The steady and regular rhythm of the stride or stroke will help you to concentrate and to become tranquilly focused in the present.

5. Clear your mind of all thoughts and concerns by concentrating intently on the flame of a candle, on trees swaying in the wind, on waves breaking.

6. Use numbers to regulate your breathing and to anchor your mind. You can choose any sequence or device you wish, in combination with your breathing or not. You can count backward, forward, by tens, or you can repeat the same numbers over and over.

7. Your meditation can revolve around a favorite prayer, hymn, saying, or passage from a book. For example, you might repeat the Serenity Prayer, or reflect on a portion of the Twenty-third Psalm.

8. Mentally transport yourself to a setting that carries pleasant and tranquil memories—a

fishing stream, a meadow filled with wild-flowers, a waterfall, a bluff overlooking the ocean.

9. In combination with any of the above techniques, you might want to experiment with a more structured and traditional form of meditation, as follows:

· Prepare your place of meditation so that it will be quiet and free of distractions; unplug the phone, close the window, put the cat out. Make it clear to everyone in the house that you are not to be disturbed, that this is your regular time for meditation. Darken the area, loosen your clothes, take off your shoes.

· Sit comfortably, with your arms and legs uncrossed and your spine straight. If you prefer, lie flat on your back on the floor, or sit cross-legged on a cushion.

· Close your eyes and let the world recede. Try to forget any problems you are having. Focus on the weight of your body as it rests on the chair or floor. Feel your body becoming heavier as you become more deeply relaxed.

· Become aware of your breathing. Your goal is to breathe slowly and deeply, from the abdomen rather than the chest.

· Beginning with your toes and moving gradually upward, relax your muscles in sequence.

Visualize the tension flowing out of your legs, arms, back, shoulders, and neck. If you have trouble releasing tension, tighten each muscle and then relax it more completely than before.

· Focus again on your slow, deep, regular breathing. With each outward breath, let go of any anxiety, fear, worry, and pain you might be carrying. With each inward breath, feel comfort and calm flowing into your body and mind.

· Once you have established the breathing rhythm that is right for you—releasing tension and bringing in tranquility—you might want to add one of the techniques mentioned earlier, such as a mantra.

· When you are completely relaxed and free of tension, open your eyes, stretch out your muscles, and affirm that you are at peace.

Quieting the Mind During Meditation

If you find that your mind tends to wander during meditation, there is no reason to feel discouraged or even concerned. Very few people are able to silence their minds completely for more than brief periods. Indeed, it's perfectly normal for all sorts of thoughts and images to filter into the consciousness.

You will probably find yourself thinking fleetingly about incompleted tasks, for example, or of pressing responsibilities. You might be revisited by old memories and forgotten fears, or you may begin to feel self-conscious and self-critical.

If this happens and you temporarily lose the focus of your meditation, don't panic. Don't even fight it. When random thoughts and speculations enter your mind during meditation, it's better not to resist, but instead to let them flow through.

This point is well made by Dr. Joan Borysenko in her book *Minding the Body, Mending the Mind.* "The most common experience and complaint about meditation is 'I can't stop my mind from wandering,'" Borysenko writes. "That's fine. Don't try. Just practice bringing it back to concentration on the breath and focus whenever you notice its wanderings. St. Francis had a great comment about wandering thoughts: You can't stop the birds from flying back and forth over your head, but you can stop them from nesting in your hair. Let the thoughts come and go as if they were birds passing across the blue sky of a clear mind. The clear blue that you will perceive when the thoughts slow down is peace. Peace of mind."

Carry the Stillness with You

Many people like to meditate in the morning. They do so not only to begin the day refreshed and tranquil, but also to establish the kind of consciousness that will enable them to go serenely about their business in the hours ahead, no matter what takes place around them.

Emphasizing this aspect of meditation to her disciples, spiritual leader Sri Daya Mata often uses an illustration that was passed on to her by her guru, Paramahansa Yogananda. "After one milks a cow, filling the pail to the brim, if he then carries it carelessly, spilling all the contents on the way to the house, there was no point in collecting the milk, because it has all been wasted. The same is true about meditation: After achieving stillness within, it is important to very carefully, watchfully carry that pail of peace with us throughout the entire day, drinking deeply from it, so that we can benefit from what we achieved in meditation."

Channeling Your Imagination

A friend once described to me a recurring childhood fantasy. When violence erupted at home, as it frequently did, he would lock himself in his bedroom, close his eyes tightly, and await the arrival of a beautiful white, winged horse.

Soon, safely astride the horse's back with his hands tucked deeply into its mane, he would soar skyward to a peaceful destination of his own choosing.

Naturally, I related to the fantasy. Don't we all occasionally use our imaginations to escape from problems or painful situations? We gaze off into the distance, visualizing ourselves in a different place at a different time, doing something highly enjoyable.

We may not realize it, but when we "get away from it all" in this way, we are using a relaxation and healing technique known as mental imagery. Many people, including my friend with the winged horse, have learned to use this liberating tool consciously and purposefully. They use it not just to "transport" themselves out of difficult situations, but also to overcome anxiety and fear, to regain a sense of control, to speed the healing process when they are ill or injured, and to achieve certain other objectives.

Mental imagery is a simple and highly effective process that you can try right away. Here's how to use it to achieve three specific goals. Feel free to augment or alter these exercises, and to apply them to other areas of your life.

I. Mental Imagery as a Stress-Reduction Tool

· Find a quiet place where you won't be disturbed. Get comfortable and try to relax.
· Close your eyes and breathe deeply and regularly. Mentally scan your body for points of tension. When you find one, relax the muscles in that area.
· Imagine that you are at the beach, standing barefooted in the warm sand. Watch the waves form in the distance, roll toward you, rise to a peak, and break. Visualize the white water as it flows in and out.
· Tune in to the sounds of the sea—the crash of surf, the cries of gulls, the noisy splashes of pelicans diving for fish.
· Watch the sandpipers as they closely follow the receding surf and frantically dig for morsels in the wet sand, then scurry to safety as the next wave breaks.
· Inhale the salt air with its pungent overtones of sea life. Feel the onshore breeze and faint salt spray ruffling your hair and cooling your face.
· Let your body and mind find the pulse of the ocean. Flow along with its currents, rhythm, and power.
· Look toward the horizon and reflect on the ocean's enormity. Visualize its depth and breadth, its globe-circling vastness. Picture other

continents, other countries, and countless other seashores being influenced by the same mighty force.

· When you feel that you are one with the timeless ebb and flow of the sea—when you are completely relaxed, renewed, and free of stress—open your eyes.

II. Mental Imagery As a Goal-Fulfillment Technique

Mental imagery also can be used effectively to prepare for and pursue positive expectations —becoming more skilled at a sport, for example; becoming more creative as a writer or musician; becoming more poised and confident in specific career or social situations. Let's say your goal is to do well at an upcoming job interview:

· Find a quiet place where you won't be disturbed. Get comfortable and try to relax.
· Close your eyes and breathe deeply and regularly. Mentally scan your body for points of tension. When you find one, relax the muscles in that area.
· Create a clear mental image of your goal, with all its positive ramifications. See yourself on the new job, doing exactly what you wish to be doing. Hold on to this image until you feel completely comfortable with it, before moving on to

the next step. If fears and doubts surface and threaten your confidence, don't resist them. Instead, allow them to flow through you, without negatively influencing your consciousness.

· Review in your mind the success you have already achieved in your field, the related experience you have had, the proven skills you can bring to the new job.

· See yourself as fully qualified and eminently capable of doing the job—as well or better than any other candidate.

· Look ahead to the actual day of the interview. You are ready to leave your house, and you are completely prepared outwardly and inwardly. You are dressed exactly right; you are unafraid, calm, and confident.

· See yourself at the interview. You are relaxed and on top of things. You are poised, outgoing, and mentally sharp.

· Visualize the person who will conduct the job interview. See him (her) not as an authority figure or someone standing in critical judgment, but as a person genuinely interested in your background, qualifications, and capabilities.

· Imagine yourself once again on the new job, well-established and completely satisfied.

· Affirm that you are going to present yourself in the best possible light, and that if you are meant to get the job you surely will.

III. Mental Imagery As a Self-Healing Tool

Mental imagery is often used as a healing technique that is adjunctive to medical care. As with exercises I and II, it can be tailored to fit your personal health needs—pain reduction, for example, or stimulation of your body's immune system to speed up recovery from illness or injury. Let's say you are recuperating from surgery and will be bedridden for a week or more:

· Close your eyes and breathe deeply and regularly. Mentally scan your body for points of tension. When you find one, relax the muscles in that area.
· To become more deeply relaxed, and to shift into the proper state of mind for self-healing, focus on pleasant times when you were fully active, when you were at your physical peak. Affirm that you will soon reach that peak again.
· Visualize the surgical site. Imagine the area becoming increasingly more supple and whole, with any tightness or inflammation steadily fading away.
· If there is pain, visualize it as an array of tiny knives directed toward you. Concentrate on reversing the knives' direction. See them leaving your body, moving rapidly away from you, traveling far beyond any capability of causing you further discomfort.

· If you feel yourself becoming tense, take the time again to relax your mind and body. Revisit your pleasant memories.

· Now imagine that your room is bathed in golden light, a light with extraordinary healing power. Absorb that light into your body, and gradually focus all of its incredible healing power on the surgical site.

· Combine the power of that golden light with the power of your body's immune system, and with every bit of healing power in the universe. Concentrate the combined healing power on the wound, a wound that is becoming ever more pain-free, healthy, and whole.

· Affirm that you are making remarkable progress, and that you will soon be in better shape than ever before. See yourself completely well, up and around again.

· Throughout the day, repeat this exercise as often as possible.

Overcoming "Brain Chatter" and Other Stress Producers

As discussed in earlier chapters, it doesn't take a four-alarm fire to get our adrenaline flowing and pulse pounding. We can become flooded with anxiety as the result of far less serious occurrences: a bounced check, a heavy work load, a broken clothes dryer. All too often, it doesn't even take an actual event to bring on stressful feelings. Our minds alone can do the job.

If you are like most people, you are probably bothered by that part of your mind (sometimes called "the committee") that chatters away incessantly and is frequently on your case. It nags and needles you, blames and criticizes you, worries and warns you, judges and scolds you.

There you are, going about your business (or maybe just barely awake in the morning), and it starts in: "You look awful; don't go into any brightly lit rooms today!" "You really blew it, and now everyone knows how stupid you are." "They don't like you, they just put up with you."

When you are receptive to that sort of negative outflow, you end up reliving past troubles, engaging in arguments with people who aren't there, and, in short, subjecting yourself to all sorts of unnecessary emotional and physical wear and tear.

In my own experience, the worst times are when my negative brain chatter combines with a concrete problem or dilemma. If I don't quickly take action to quiet my mind, I can easily get into real trouble. The mounting stress can cause not only anxiety and mental confusion, but also physical symptoms ranging from a throbbing headache to insomnia.

When you begin to feel anxious—when you become aware of shallow breathing, deep sighs, racing thoughts, and increasing physical tension —there is no need to passively suffer through the onslaught. There are literally dozens of actions you can take to become more comfortable and serene. Here are a variety of tried-and-true relaxation techniques that can be used anytime and anywhere:

1. *Sensory awareness to anchor you in the now.* Sit in a straight-backed chair or stand against a wall and close your eyes. Allow your senses to come fully alive. Tune in to the very real world surrounding you. What do you hear? Which sounds are the loudest, softest, most rhythmic? What odors can you identify? Food? Perfume? Smoke? Chemicals? Now open your eyes. What do you see *here and now*? What is actually occurring in your world?

2. *Focus on your breathing.* Your mind can deal with only one thing at a time. If you keep it occupied by concentrating on your incoming and outgoing breaths, it won't be able to overpower you with negative, stress-producing thoughts. Become aware of the rhythm and origin of your breathing. If it is rapid, consciously slow it; if it is shallow, consciously deepen it.

3. *Talk to someone.* Pick up the phone and call someone you are close to, preferably an understanding friend or family member. If there's no answer, try another person. Once you've contacted someone, don't beat around the bush; tell him or her exactly what's bothering you and how you feel. Very often, relief from anxiety will come in the "telling."

4. *Stretch away stress.* Mental tension usually brings on physical tension. You can turn the tables: by becoming physically relaxed, you can unwind mentally and emotionally. Zero in on the five major areas where tension is stored—the face, neck, shoulders, back, and chest. Work on these areas one at a time, repeatedly stretching the muscle groups until you feel tension draining away.

5. *Visualization as preparation.* If anticipation of an upcoming event or responsibility (a dreaded phone call, a presentation, a confrontation) is causing you anxiety, mentally "rehearse" in advance. Relax as much as possible, then picture yourself going through the potentially stressful event step-by-step—smoothly, calmly, and with an abundance of positive energy. This sort of preparation can go a long way toward reducing anxiety, because you will gain a more

realistic sense of what to expect, what to say, and how to act.

6. *Screen your mind's messages.* When your mind begins to attack you—when negative brain chatter begins to whip you into an emotional frenzy—commit yourself to taking a stand. Affirm that you are in control of your mind, rather than the other way around.

As best you can, slow down the pace of your thoughts and physical movements. Then try to objectively observe and evaluate your mind's messages to you. Is the message true or false? Is the intent constructive or destructive? Does the message deserve a reaction, or should it be replaced with one that is more accurate, positive, and healthy?

7. *Physical exercise.* If time and circumstances permit, exercise (walking, running, cycling, racquetball, the choice is yours) is an ideal way to settle down and become anchored in the present. While calming your mind, exercise also encourages you to breathe deeply and evenly. By diverting your attention from whatever has been bothering you, it will also change your perspective and mood. Moreover, exercise can give you a sense of euphoria—the so-called "natural high" that is brought on by the body's release of endorphins.

8. *Turning to God for peace.* No matter where you are and what is going on inside you or around you, thoughts of God can bring reassurance and help you become peaceful and centered again. Even if you are unable to pray or meditate, try to be still. Allow God's love to flow into you, replacing turmoil with tranquility.

Listening to Your Inner Voice

In addition to our five physical senses—our ability to see, hear, smell, touch, and taste—we all have a "sixth sense" of intuition. Intuition has been described as the special wisdom, beyond intellect or ego, that guides us into right decisions and actions.

The foundation of intuition is inner stillness. The exercises in this chapter, singly or in combination, can create that foundation and put you in the best possible position to listen to and trust your inner voice.

You may feel that you have very little of this sixth sense. But intuition can be developed. Just as your muscles or limbs are gradually strengthened by exercise, your intuitive voice will grow stronger as you regularly take actions to still your mind.

Intuition expresses itself in various ways, and is, of course, a uniquely personal experience.

It may come to you in the form of a strong gut feeling, as an image in your mind's eye, or as a physical sensation sweeping through your body. Some people experience an actual "rush." You may be intuitively guided by the words or actions of another person, by the way events unfold or circumstances fall into place, or even by subtle "vibrations" that are hard to describe.

While your intuition is a part of you that can be enhanced and amplified, so to speak, it can also be easily drowned out. It's difficult to feel or hear the urgings of your inner voice when you are agitated, irritable, restless, or rushed. Think about it. Isn't it true that you tend to become confused and make wrong decisions when you are tired and emotionally overwrought? On the other hand, don't you frequently *know* what to do when you are calm and poised?

Intuition can also be drowned out by the louder and more insistent voice of ego and self-will. When this happens, the inner voice whispers, "Don't do it—it's wrong for you," but willfulness tries to lead you astray by shouting, "This is what you want. Go ahead, you can handle it!"

It's sometimes difficult to differentiate between those conflicting voices. In my own case, on occasion I want something so badly that I delude myself into thinking that it is right for me, that it is meant to be, and that the voice of my ego is in fact my intuitive voice.

So it is a continuing goal to become more sensitive to my caring, protective inner voice, and to develop greater trust in its guidance. I must say that my inner voice is strongest and most persuasive when I am close to God, praying and meditating regularly.

As you learn to trust your inner voice and follow its urgings, you will be better able to recognize life's patterns and to flow along with them. You will become more spontaneous and creative, in tune with your own natural inclinations.

As your inner voice grows stronger, you will become increasingly aware of possibilities and opportunities you didn't know existed. Decisions will come easily; you will intuitively know how to handle situations and choices that once confounded you. In times of crisis, you will be less likely to panic or run away. More often than not, you will know exactly what to do and say.

12

Selfless and Serene

If you want to become upset and unhappy, sit down and think about yourself. Think about the opportunities you have let slip by, the misjudgments you have made, the foolish things you have said and done. Focus on your body and see if you can find a new pain or blemish to worry about. Dwell on the ways you have been mistreated. List all the things you want that you don't have, and hold fast to the idea that you won't find peace until you get them.

If, on the other hand, you want to become fulfilled and serene, sit down, relax, and think about ways to gain freedom from the bondage of self. Remind yourself that the world does not revolve around you, but that you are one among many. Ask yourself if your problems are truly as large and pressing as they seem to be, and if it isn't time to take yourself less seriously.

Find the willingness to let go of your resentments, to forgive and forget. Make a commitment to put all you can into the present moment. Think about the blessings you've received, and the power of God's love in your life. Ask yourself what you can do today to help someone else, and then do it.

Clearly, self-centeredness can be a formidable obstacle on the road to inner peace. It is at the root of many of our daily living problems, and causes anxiety and confusion that often is more troublesome than that brought on by actual calamities.

Self-centeredness is reflected in our attitudes and behavior, taking the form of such character defects as pride, envy, self-pity, lust, greed, anger, perfectionism, and jealousy. Because we're not getting our own way, we become angry. Because we're overly concerned with how we measure up to others, we become envious. Because we fear that we won't get what we want, or will lose what we have, we become greedy and possessive.

Self-centered behavior takes many forms, some glaringly obvious and some quite subtle. Whatever the case, many people have a hard time recognizing their self-centeredness and the extent to which it governs their lives.

The Many Faces of Self-centeredness

Let's take a look at some common manifestations of self-centeredness. Beginning with the obvious, self-involved people rarely express genuine interest in others, but instead focus conversations on themselves. Virtually every sentence begins with "I" and ends with "me."

Going further, they see and assimilate almost everything that happens in terms of how it affects them—how it will help them, how it will hurt them, how it will make them appear. When a family member becomes ill or incapacitated, for example, self-centered people tend to think primarily about how *they* will be inconvenienced.

Other obvious traits of self-centered people are their incessant demands, their preoccupation with unmet expectations, and their overall insatiability. For such people there is never enough love, attention, or approval. Not surprisingly, their relationships with others are invariably tumultuous, discordant, and disappointing.

At the subtle end of the scale, people who are self-centered tend to take most things in their lives (especially themselves) far too seriously. Just about everything is a "big deal," from their jobs, social status, and possessions to such run-of-the-mill variables as changes in the weather.

In disagreements, or even friendly discussions, such people always have to be "right." Whatever the subject, and no matter how limited their knowledge and experience, they present themselves as experts.

Along the same lines, people with a high degree of self-involvement usually are preoccupied with their appearance, and are overly concerned with what others think of them. They tend to see themselves as exceptional—at least to the extent that "their case is different"—so they frequently bend or break rules as it suits them.

One of the most damaging yet frequently overlooked expressions of self-centeredness is self-pity. This character flaw, which we all suffer from time to time, ranks with resentment, guilt, and fear as a surefire destroyer of inner peace.

When we retreat into self-pity we sometimes do so to avoid responsibility. We don't have to look at ourselves honestly; we don't have to acknowledge or deal with the feelings that are troubling us; we don't have to admit our wrongs, or seek solutions. Moreover, when we are under the influence of self-pity, we lose our ability to accept criticism. We may become defensive to the point of touchiness, falling to pieces at the slightest provocation.

For all of these reasons, self-pity is often compared to quicksand. The longer we wallow in it and the deeper we sink, the more difficult it is to pull ourselves out and set things right again.

To sum up, it's as simple as this: When we are filled with self, and, as the result of our flaring character defects, treat others with impatience, unkindness, intolerance, and hostility, we become anxious, guilt-ridden, and remorseful.

On the other hand, when we take actions to become self*less*, and treat others with patience, kindness, understanding, and love, we feel good about ourselves and gain a sense of inner tranquility.

REMEMBER

· Self-centeredness can slow and even block our progress toward inner peace.
· Self-centeredness expresses itself in the form of specific character flaws, some obvious, some less so.
· Of all the forms of self-centeredness, self-pity—the ''poor me'' syndrome—is one of the most destructive.
· There's no underestimating the importance of recognizing our self-centered behavior and understanding its negative impact on our lives.

It Starts with Self-awareness

You may be thinking at this point, "All I've just read makes sense, and I can certainly see myself in some of it. But aren't we all self-centered to one degree or another? Frankly, I do have certain traits I'm not especially proud of, but I've had them all my life. They're just part of me. Yes, I'd like to become less self-centered in order to become more serene, but I don't know if it's possible. I wouldn't know what to do, or where to begin."

The first step in becoming free of self-centeredness, and the character flaws born of it, is self-awareness. Before we chose a new path in life, many of us had only a vague idea of why we felt and behaved as we did. So we remained locked in unvarying patterns of thinking and acting. We eventually learned that self-awareness is essential to change and growth.

Some people develop self-awareness through counseling or therapy. Others learn about their character assets and liabilities through the personal inventories they take in Twelve Step programs. In addition to these in-depth approaches, there are numerous other ways to uncover and discover who we are, and why we feel and act as we do. Here are some techniques you may want to use:

1. *Learn from others.* When the opportunity presents itself, listen carefully as others talk about their feelings and behavior patterns. See if you can identify with their experiences, and try to apply what you learn. Talk about yourself, and remain open to any feedback you receive. Also, you may want to regularly read books and articles that lead to self-discovery.

2. *When agitated, look inward rather than outward.* Whenever you become upset, try to determine the real problem. Instead of automatically looking for someone or something to blame for the anger or hurt you feel, try to identify those character flaws within you that may be causing the problem.

Let's say someone teases you or "lords it over you," and as a result you become highly insulted, or even enraged. Instead of focusing resentfully on the person who has "harmed" you, try to uncover any traits within yourself that may be a more significant cause of your emotional flare-up. Could it be your oversensitivity, self-consciousness, or insecurity? Do you take yourself too seriously? Are you overly defensive, and quick to develop grudges?

3. *Pay attention to your insights.* From time to time you are bound to have flashes of insight about yourself. We all do. Suddenly and with

great clarity, for example, you may be able to see connections between past influences and present behavior; to tie specific events to subsequent periods of depression; to recognize previously undiscovered character flaws; or to become sharply aware of recent selfish and dishonest behavior.

More often than not, these intuitive awarenesses are at first painful, or they may make you uncomfortable. You may be tempted to rebury them, or to simply ignore them. However, such insights can be valuable sources of information about yourself—all the more so if you *act* on them.

4. *Observe your actions and interactions.* Another good way to become more self-aware is to periodically step outside of yourself, so to speak, in order to objectively observe your attitudes, motives, and behavior in various situations.

When you are involved with others, for example, you might try to determine if your primary concern is the impression you are making on them, or whether you are being sensitive to their needs. At work, you might monitor your disposition. Are you carrying around negative emotions and giving off negative energy? Or are you doing the best job you can and trying to get along with your associates? And what about the way you treat yourself? Are you constantly on your own case, being unmercifully critical? Or are you trying to be gentle, supportive, and loving?

If you observe yourself in these ways over a period of time, you may become aware of long-standing behavioral patterns that have been causing you inner disquiet.

5. *Include self-assessment in your daily routine.* Because it can be easy to fall back into patterns of self-deception, many people take a brief personal inventory at the end of each day. You can begin your self-survey by going over the day's events, focusing on your feelings, attitudes, actions, and reactions.

Your goal is not to judge or chastise yourself, but to gain self-awareness. If, for example, you find that you have not been living up to your goals and values, that awareness can be a starting point for positive changes. Daily self-assessments are highly practical; they can show you where you have been, where you need to go, and what you need to do to get there.

Whatever tools and techniques you use, learning about yourself is an ongoing process. Hopefully, you will become increasingly self-aware day after day and year after year throughout your life. More important, if you act on your awarenesses—striving to temper the character defects and to eliminate the destructive behavioral patterns that lead to living problems—you will become more and more peaceful within.

In other words, self-awareness is only part of the growth process. Your awarenesses, no matter how revealing, can be maximized only when you become willing to change and then take decisive actions to do so.

REMEMBER

Self-awareness provides you with choices. It's up to you to make them.

God Can Do for You What You Can't Do for Yourself

If your experience has been anything like mine, for years you tried to get rid of your character defects—with little success. Changing yourself may *still* seem like a complicated and impossible undertaking. You may even have resigned yourself to the idea that certain unyielding traits will forever cause you confusion, self-doubt, and heartache.

That's the way I felt for a long time. I would grit my teeth, clench my fists, and try with all my power to change the things about myself that were causing me pain and disrupting my life. Time after time I would fail. Then I would strengthen my resolve and try again, once more relying solely on my own willpower to achieve the desired results.

My efforts were totally self-defeating. The harder I tried, the more frustrating were my failures, and the less faith I had in my ability to change my flawed attitudes and behavior.

Eventually, during the early years of my recovery, I was taught this humbling and life-altering truth: *While I may not be able to bring about change in myself, faith in God's ability to do so, along with willingness rather than more willpower, does enable me to change greatly.*

To elaborate, this was the sequence of actions presented to me:

• With personal inventory and other techniques to develop self-awareness, work toward uncovering and identifying your character defects and the harmful behavioral patterns they cause.
• Become completely willing to have those defects and patterns removed. Look deep into your heart and ask yourself if you are truly ready to let go of the selfishness, for example, that has been such a powerful motivational force in your life.
• Turn to God and ask Him, with faith and humility, to remove your character defects.

• Act in faith by doing "the footwork." That is, ask God to remove the defect of selfishness, but also do your part by being as thoughtful and considerate as you can.

This may sound like a lofty and far too theoretical approach to painful personal problems—the kind that can cause you to wring your hands in anguish or to shout out in frustration. But it really does work, and thousands upon thousands of people the world over have come to rely on it.

To see how these actions can work in your life, take a few moments to put yourself into this typical scenario:

Your boyfriend (girlfriend) has some business dealings with his (her) ex-spouse. You become jealous and suspicious, even though the feelings are unwarranted. Before long, you are obsessed with your irrational fears.

You try and try to be objective about the situation and to let go, but you can't shake your consuming jealousy. Finally, after beating yourself to an emotional pulp, you see the futility of relying on willpower alone to set yourself free.

There's no question that you are entirely ready to be rid of the character flaw—your jealousy. So you put your faith in God and humbly ask Him to remove it. Following that, you try to act in such a way that you are, in effect, working along with God.

You keep busy, and concentrate on the present moment. When jealous thoughts flare, you try to replace them with positive ones: the trust you and your partner have shared for so long; God's love; the blessings in your life. After a time, you realize that you are no longer caught in the web of obsession. Your jealousy has been lifted, and you are back to your old self.

Once you try out these spiritual tools—on a particular character defect, obsession, or compulsion—and find that God can indeed do for you what you haven't been able to do for yourself, you'll be encouraged to apply them in other areas. As your life gradually changes for the better, your faith will deepen and your trust will grow stronger.

It goes without saying that few character defects ever disappear entirely. Some do fade in a relatively short time, but others are less yielding. After all, most behavioral patterns have evolved over a lifetime; you can't expect to put all of them behind you once and for all.

Moreover, you may sometimes be tempted to resurrect certain character defects when you sense they might be useful. You throw a tantrum, for example, to get attention. You become manipulative to get your own way. You indulge in self-pity to avoid responsibility.

However, if you regularly apply the spiritual tools described above, over time your character defects will surface less frequently, and when they do they won't be as intense or last as long.

As your tolerance for emotional pain decreases and your willingness to ask for God's help grows, you will more quickly move from the problem into the solution.

Out of Self, into Service

Just as self-centeredness can be a major obstacle on the road to inner peace, service to others can be a bridge to that destination.

How, exactly, can we cross that bridge? Some people think they are not in a position to "be of service" because they lack the time and financial means. When they think about service, they think about the rich and famous—people who have opportunities to donate large sums of money and special talents to various causes. Others think they may not be "spiritually evolved" enough to be of service.

Of course, such views do not reflect reality. Our giving need not be material in nature. The essence of service is offering others what means the most to us: kindness, understanding, empathy, and love. Therefore, each of us can be of service in our everyday life—in the way we interact with our fellows; in how we treat our friends, co-workers, family members, even strangers.

Whatever we do, wherever we go, whomever we're with, there are always countless opportunities to be generous of heart. We can be of service (and in so doing, get out of ourselves) by listening attentively to others and showing interest in their lives. We can offer approval, encouragement, and hope; we can be courteous and complimentary. Sometimes a warm smile can turn around another person's day.

In my own experience, I've learned that I'm the one who benefits most when I go out of my way to help someone else. This is especially true when I'm in emotional pain, when I've lost perspective, and when life seems unfair. Such simple acts as calling a friend to see how he is feeling, or introducing myself to a newly recovering alcoholic, invariably helps me to climb out of myself, to see my problems right size, and to feel good about life again.

For years I had an entirely different view about giving. In my view, and it certainly seemed axiomatic, the more you gave away, the less you had for yourself. Wasn't that the whole point of life—to grab and accumulate as much as you could, and do whatever was necessary to keep it?

On those infrequent occasions when I did offer to help another person in some way, it was with the expectation that I would get something in return.

The paradox was that my self-serving behavior led not to enrichment of any kind, but rather to an all-encompassing sense of emptiness and uselessness. What I've come to understand is that giving means getting. The more I give, the more I receive.

REMEMBER

· Service to others can lift you out of yourself and further your progress to inner peace.
· Whatever you do, wherever you go, whomever you're with, there are countless opportunities each day to reach out to others.
· Generosity of heart—an attentive ear, an encouraging word—can mean more than grand gestures or material gifts.
· Giving of yourself enhances rather than diminishes you.

Benchmarks of Progress

As you make progress in these areas—as you become more self-aware and less self-centered; as you strive to become free of your character flaws; as you think about others and give of yourself—you will move toward humility.

· You will become open, teachable, and willing to learn. You will be able to say, "I don't know," and to benefit from other people's knowledge and experience.
· You will gain a quiet awareness and acceptance of who you are. You will lose the need to measure up, to stand out, to influence and impress.
· You will think less about yourself and your limited objectives, and more about others and God.
· You will be able to honestly and accurately assess yourself, your limitations as well as your capabilities. When you face adversity, or a character defect flares, you will recognize the need to seek help from a Power greater than yourself.
· You will be grateful for what you have, and feel secure in the faith that God will always provide for you.
· You will know peace.

13

Summary: Pathways to Inner Peace

Chapter 1: Introduction: From Turmoil to Tranquility

· To know inner peace is to be in harmony with the world around you, flowing along with life's natural order, believing that every occurrence (not only the obviously good, but also the seemingly bad) has a purpose and is part of a Divine plan.

· To know inner peace is to live in accordance with your true self, with no need for posturing or pretensions, free of the past, without guilt, resentment, or blame, present in the here and now, with the desire and capability of enjoying life to its fullest.

· True and lasting inner peace can never be

found in external things. It can only be found
within.
• People who are at peace with themselves not
only have a deep sense of personal well-being,
but also tend to be physically healthier. Medical
researchers have demonstrated that there is a
clear link between stress and illness.
• Your anxiety-producing attitudes, reactions,
and behavior are habitual and even second nature. To live peacefully, it's essential to replace
the old ways with new, life-affirming attitudes
and reactions. Inner peace will come as the direct
result of the way you live your life—the values
you honor, the choices you make, and the actions you take.

Chapter 2:   Altered Attitudes

• Attitude is all-important. As much as anything else, it determines how you experience
each moment, each hour, each day.
• Nobody can force you to feel or act a certain
way. You may be limited in your ability to
change the outside event (be it a delayed flight
or a neighbor's unkind remark), but you have
unlimited ability to choose your own attitude
and reaction.
• Each morning, when you awaken, you have
the opportunity to choose the attitude and set

the emotional tone that will largely determine how you experience the day ahead.

· You also have unlimited opportunities to adjust your attitude. Whatever the hour, wherever you are, no matter what you are doing, you can start again.

· By objectively observing your mind's "messages" over a period of time, you can discover what negative beliefs you are holding. As you gain awareness of your thoughts and how they affect you, you will gradually learn to control your mind rather than passively allow it to control you.

· Judgmental attitudes keep you in a stressful state. When you constantly judge others, you are likely to feel that you yourself are being judged in the same way; you become self-conscious and self-critical.

· Here are some effective techniques to help you transform negative attitudes into positive ones and gain serenity:

1. Do what you can to regain perspective and see everything—especially yourself—right size.

2. When something has upset you and your deteriorating attitude is ruining your day, honestly answer the question "How important is it?"

3. Readjust your attitude by phoning a friend, by taking an exercise break, by meditating, or with any other action that works for you.

4. Take a moment to make a mental or written list of all you have to be grateful for.

5. Move out of the problem and into the solution by listing and then following through with constructive options.

6. Turn your thoughts to God. Ask yourself how your Creator would have you think and act.

Chapter 3: Savor the Moment, Seize the Day

· When you are living fully in the now, that's when you are the most peaceful and fulfilled.

· If your happiness and tranquility is contingency-oriented, depending on something you expect to happen in the future, you miss out on the joys and satisfactions available in the here and now.

· At this moment you are exactly where you are supposed to be—where God and your past actions have led you. The more accepting you are of that reality, the more inner peace you are likely to have.

· Mental projection forward into the future, or backward into the past, is almost always a distortion of reality. It is powered by fear and guilt, and invariably causes anxiety.

· By choosing simplicity—not only in your daily living routines, but in your personal goals overall—you can gain more control over your life and achieve greater inner peace.

· Here are some exercises that can help you stay anchored in the present moment:

1. Practice "being present" in everything you do. When your mind wanders, actively bring it back.

2. Stay committed to your decisions; don't second-guess yourself.

3. Take brief "centering" breaks throughout the day.

4. Anchor your mind by focusing on God, or on the sound and rhythm of your own breathing.

5. Live a day at a time, resolving to deal only with what is put in front of you.

6. Begin each day with a commitment to stay in the now.

Chapter 4: People, Places, Things: The Paradox of Control

· You have a certain amount of control as far as your own attitudes, perspectives, and reactions are concerned. But in other areas—those involving people, institutions, and events—you frequently are powerless.

· When you fail to accept your powerlessness and willfully insist on "doing battle," you are bound to pay a heavy price in the form of emotional and physical stress.

· You can accept your powerlessness and preserve your serenity by: a) doing everything you can to remedy the situation; b) letting it go by turning it over to God; c) getting on with your life.

· You can learn to recognize the areas where you truly lack control by looking carefully at all your relationships, at your day-to-day work and leisure patterns, and at all aspects of your life that are potentially frustrating. Then, whenever you feel anxious or upset, ask yourself: Am I trying to fight, resist, or preserve something over which I have no control?

· Acceptance allows you to live life on life's terms—taking people, circumstances, and events as they are, rather than as you wish them to be.

· Acceptance can bring immediate relief from problems that seem overwhelming. The practice of this dynamic spiritual principle can quiet your inner turmoil and help you transcend your difficulties, no matter what the circumstances.

· Much of the friction and strain in relationships occurs when we try to manage and control others, expecting them to conform to our concept of how they should be.

· Even if your motives are positive in trying to change or "cure" another person, you are bound to be unsuccessful. Nobody changes until he or she is willing to change and takes actions to do so.

· When we insist on managing and controlling others, we deprive them of the opportunity to learn from their own choices and mistakes.

· As you begin to practice detachment (learning to "live and let live"), you can be empathetic and supportive while respecting the right of another to find his or her own way.

· Just because you are powerless over someone or something and have become willing to step aside, that doesn't mean that the situation is hopeless. You "let go and let God" with the conviction that somehow, in some way, positive change will take place.

Chapter 5: A Power Greater Than Yourself

· True and lasting inner fulfillment, and the emotional stability and serenity that come with it, can be found in a spiritual way of life.

· Belief in a Power greater than yourself can bring order and purpose to a world that often seems chaotic and unfair. With God as a constant source of strength and good in your life, you will be free to do things that previously were impossible.

· Neither fear, disillusionment, nor agnosticism need stand in your way on the path to spirituality. To move forward, all you need to do is open your mind and admit that you do not have all the answers.

· No matter what your background or what your past experiences have been, you are free to seek a God *of your own understanding*. You don't have to conform to other people's beliefs or concepts.

· One of the best ways to develop an ever-stronger relationship with your Higher Power is through prayer and meditation. Prayer is the way we talk to God; meditation is the way we listen to Him.

· For faith to become a useful part of your life, it must be practiced and applied. Each time you turn to God for guidance and courage, and He comes through, your faith is strengthened.

· At any time of the day or night, no matter what is taking place around you or within you, you can always regain a sense of calm by centering your thoughts on God.

Chapter 6: Surrendering to Win

· When we "surrender to win," we stop trying to overcome a problem by relying solely on our own limited resources. We place the problem in God's hands, trusting that He will solve it in the best way possible.

· Even if you have been conditioned to believe that there is something negative about "giving up," consider this: By allowing God to do for you what you cannot do for yourself, you will become victorious through surrender.

· In the interest of lasting serenity, you can use the tool of surrender almost without limitation. The way to begin is by making a daily commitment to stop fighting everything and everyone.

· As your tolerance for pain and frustration decreases, your willingness to surrender will increase.

· If most of the time you feel serene and in harmony with others and the world around you, these are good indications that you are following God's will. But if you are usually in conflict—if you frequently feel anxious, impatient, and out of sorts—these are good indications that you are living primarily by self-will.

· When we have humility, we see ourselves in proper perspective. Humility allows us to abandon our own limited objectives, surrender to

God, and move toward His perfect objectives for us.

· The transition from willfulness and total self-reliance to humility and reliance on God certainly isn't an overnight process. It takes place day by day, through patient effort and a relaxed sense of surrender to your Higher Power.

Chapter 7: Faith-filled and Fear-less

· When we face actual danger, fear provides us with the decisiveness, quickness, and strength we need to protect ourselves. But groundless or irrational fear is highly destructive, capable of negatively influencing our decisions and literally shaping our lives.

· Few people have any real idea of how much fear they carry and of the extent to which this emotion erodes their self-esteem, keeps them stuck in emotional ruts, and ruins their health.

· Our fears sometimes disguise themselves as other "more acceptable" emotions, ranging from jealousy and anger to greed and intolerance.

· We have to first become aware of our fears, and to acknowledge how they are negatively affecting our lives, before we can take steps to undo the damage they cause.

· Learning to embrace change is one of the keys to inner peace. Think back to one or more changes you feared and resisted strongly, and to the inner turmoil you needlessly suffered as the result.

· Whenever you are afraid, you can find courage, strength, and confidence by replacing fear with faith—by reminding yourself that you are surrounded by God's love and protection.

· Here are some effective methods for overcoming fear:

1. Look beyond the fear for the facts. Ask yourself, "Is it *really* as frightening as it seems?"

2. Talk it out.

3. Approach fearful situations as challenges to be met, as opportunities to grow, as adventures to be experienced.

4. Look behind fear's disguises.

5. Visualize the outcome, including the worst possible scenario, and ask yourself: Can I handle it?

6. Walk through the fear a minute at a time, an hour at a time, a day at a time.

7. Replace fear with faith, reminding yourself of the previous times God has seen you through.

Chapter 8: Getting Rid of Excess Baggage

· Most people carry around a heavy load of resentment, guilt, and remorse stemming from unresolved issues of the past. This "excess baggage" is responsible for much inner turmoil. Until we come to terms with the past, it will remain a volatile source of anguish and fear.

· Resentments, which comprise the weightiest portion of most people's excess baggage, are highly damaging—physically, emotionally, and spiritually. Resentments cause stress and illness, keep you raw and vulnerable, lead to obsession, and chain you to the past.

· It is absolutely essential to get rid of your resentments, no matter what their origin or focus. Even when you are convinced that your resentment is entirely justified, you still must let it go in the interest of inner peace.

· Here are steps you can take to become free of this poisonous emotion:

1. Think about how your resentment is harming you, while the person you resent is completely unaware and unaffected.

2. Write out a "grudge list" of your resentments, and you will see how pointless most of them are.

3. Look within to see if your behavior may have contributed to the problem. Pray for the person you resent, and ask God to remove your resentments.

· Forgiveness is a powerful force for healing and growth: it extinguishes the embers of resentment; it allows you to salvage and rebuild relationships; it furthers spiritual progress by encouraging you to practice understanding, acceptance, and compassion.

· Of all the emotions that keep people chained to the past, none is more corrosive to self-esteem or causes more inner turmoil than guilt. To travel smoothly and successfully toward your goal of inner peace, you must do so without this toxic burden.

· Here are actions you can take to rid yourself of lingering guilt and become free of the past:

1. Bring the past out into the open by writing and talking about the unresolved, guilt-provoking issues that are still causing you pain.

2. Make amends for past wrongs.

3. Forgive yourself, and ask for God's forgiveness.

4. Live a quality life today. In all of your affairs strive to be honest, tolerant, kind, loving, responsible, and giving.

· While you are coming to terms with the past, it is important to live in such a way that you don't allow new excess baggage to accumulate. Here are some ways to keep the decks clear:

1. Deal with negative emotions, especially anger, as soon as they surface.

2. Remain honest and aboveboard. Remem-

ber that dishonesty of any kind can only complicate your life.

3. Avoid procrastination and keep your affairs in order.

4. Promptly admit your wrongs and mistakes.

5. At the end of each day, identify unresolved issues, then commit yourself to taking care of them quickly.

Chapter 9: The Others in Our Lives

· Relationships can bring us joy and fulfillment, while also providing opportunities to learn about ourselves and to grow. But relationships can also cause great emotional pain and stress.

· Healthy relationships require time and effort; the willingness to accept others just as they are; open and honest communications; mutual respect; and active, unconditional love.

· When we unrealistically expect another person to bring us the peace and security that can only come from within ourselves, the relationship will likely fail.

· To build harmonious relationships, we must concentrate on strengthening our own inner resources, instead of expecting others to fill our empty spaces and "make us right" through their actions.

· The soundest relationships are built on a foundation of healthy interdependence—that is, mutual trust and caring. The goals are to work out and exchange solutions; help one another grow emotionally and spiritually; and give the best of ourselves to each other, without expecting anything in return.

· When communications in relationships are blocked, the emotional toll can be devastating. On the other hand, nothing quite matches the sense of stability and well-being that comes when communications are honest, clear, and free-flowing.

· Here are some tools and techniques that can improve communications in your relationships:

1. Keep the channels open.

2. Take the initiative in resolving conflicts.

3. Develop listening skills and put them to use.

4. Avoid mixed messages and hidden agendas.

5. Eliminate sarcasm and teasing.

· True love is active love, and its flow is more outward than inward. It is when you are most loving to others that love grows strongest within yourself.

Chapter 10: Solitulde

· Solitude is an important component of inner tranquility. It allows you to rediscover and reaffirm the ideas and emotions that define your true and natural self.

· The more self-acceptance you have, the more peaceful you will be during times of solitude, and the more benefits you will receive.

· Self-acceptance means embracing all of yourself, not just the "good stuff." It means honoring and loving yourself exactly as you are, at this very moment.

· If you tend to become uncomfortable and "itchy" even during short periods of solitude, you can develop a taste for it and benefit from it by:

1. Scheduling time to be alone.

2. Approaching your "experimental" periods of solitude with an open mind.

3. Explaining to family members why you need time to be alone.

4. Remembering that your goal during solitude is not to "get things done," or to grit your teeth through a period of boredom.

Chapter 11: An Inner Stillness, An Inner Healing

· The whole idea of self-renewal activity is to withdraw into yourself, to restore your energy and inner spirit, and to bring harmony and stability to your life.

· Through meditation, you can achieve inner stillness. With mental imagery, you can overcome apprehension and other stressful feelings. By applying a variety of relaxation techniques, you can become physically and emotionally renewed.

· By meditating, you can deepen your consciousness of God and open yourself to His guidance and inspiration. Meditation will also help you find and listen to your intuitive voice and gain serenity.

· Meditation is an entirely individual process. You need not concern yourself with whether you meditate "properly"; meditation can be whatever you want it to be.

· If your mind tends to wander during meditation, don't panic or even resist. When random thoughts and speculations enter your mind, let them flow through.

· Mental imagery is a liberating tool that can be used to overcome anxiety and fear; to regain a sense of control; to prepare for and pursue positive expectations; and to speed the healing process.

· There are literally dozens of actions you can take to overcome stress and become more comfortable and relaxed. Here are several that can be used anytime and anywhere:

1. Anchor yourself in the present moment by tuning in to the sights, sounds, and odors of the real world surrounding you.

2. Focus on your breathing.

3. Talk to someone.

4. Stretch the muscle groups where tension is stored.

5. Mentally "rehearse" an upcoming event that is causing you anxiety. That way, you can gain a realistic sense of what to expect, what to say, and how to act.

6. Screen your mind's messages. Replace negative thoughts with more accurate, positive, and healthy ones.

7. Do some physical exercise.

8. Turn to God for peace.

· Intuition is a special wisdom, beyond intellect or ego, that can guide you into right decisions and actions. Your intuitive voice will grow stronger as you regularly take actions to still your mind.

Chapter 12: *Selfless and Serene*

· Self-centeredness can be a major obstacle on the road to tranquility. It causes anxiety and confusion, and is at the root of many of our daily living problems.

· Self-centered attitudes and behavior take many forms, some obvious and some subtle. Many people have a hard time recognizing their self-centeredness and the extent to which it governs their lives.

· The first step in becoming free of self-centeredness, and the character flaws born of it, is self-awareness—that is, discovering and understanding why you feel and act as you do.

· In addition to in-depth personal inventories and perhaps professional counseling, there are other techniques that can help you become more self-aware:

 1. Learn from others.

 2. When agitated, try to identify the character flaws within you that may be causing the problem.

 3. Pay attention to your insights about yourself, and try to act on them.

 4. Observe your actions and interactions with others.

 5. Include self-assessment in your daily routine.

· While it is important to act on your aware-nesses, it isn't always possible to bring about the change in yourself that you desire. When you are entirely ready to be rid of a character flaw or a destructive behavioral pattern, you can put your faith in God and humbly ask Him to remove it. Then you can try to act in such a way that you are, in effect, working along with God.

· Service to others is an antidote to self-centeredness and the inner turmoil it causes. Each day there are countless opportunities to be generous of heart. The more you help others, the more you benefit yourself; the more you give, the more you receive.

Appendix:

Self-assessment Survey

1. Do you believe that inner peace will come when you finally have enough money, the career you want, or that "special someone" in your life? Or have you begun to understand that true and lasting inner peace is an inside job?

2. Have you begun to recognize that much of your inner turmoil is generated by your own attitudes, reactions, and behavior? Or do you still automatically blame other people, places, and things for your fear, worry, and anger?

3. Do you frequently see yourself as a "victim of circumstances," blaming outside forces for your anxiety and unhappiness? Or have you begun to accept responsibility for your feelings and reactions?

4. If you awaken with feelings of apprehension or even dread, do you allow those feelings to taint everything you do during the day? Or do you lie quietly for a few moments and try to replace those negative feelings with positive ones, and to shape a new frame of mind?

5. When a series of negative thoughts begins to drag you downhill, do you passively go along on the punishing ride? Or do you hold your ground and reverse the process by immediately occupying your mind with positive reflections?

6. Do you still think it's okay to judge or tease others as long as it's in the spirit of "fun"? Or do you realize that judgmentalism is a character defect as harmful to you as those you judge?

7. When a friend or loved one is upset, disdainful, or hostile, do you absorb their negative feelings? Or do you exercise your power of choice—sending forth positive energy of your own to offset the negative energy coming your way?

8. Do you live for the day when an expected or hoped-for future event will finally bring you peace of mind? Or do you try to fully accept and make the most of your life today?

9. Are you troubled by a "vocabulary of anxiety"? Do you constantly jolt yourself with

such admonishing and fearsome phrases as "What if . . . ?" "If only . . ." "Could've . . ." "Should've . . ."? Or are you learning to counteract your mind's tendency to take you to places you don't want to go?

10. Are you often stirred up and anxious about time constraints—lack of time, time wasted, time lost? Or are you replacing that concept by seeing and using time as a numerical system that can be your ally rather than your enemy?

11. When you are facing decisions and making new choices, do you tend to act impulsively, without thought for long-term consequences? Or do you try to determine beforehand how your choices will affect your physical, emotional, and spiritual well-being?

12. Do you still exhaust yourself physically and emotionally by stubbornly trying to exercise power that was never yours to begin with? Or are you finding ways to preserve your inner peace, while allowing events to run their course?

13. Have you experienced the joy and relief that comes with a deep-down acknowledgment of powerlessness?

14. Do you practice acceptance only in "serious" matters? Or are you finding that it can be applied to any and all situations beyond your

control, including the relatively minor frustrations we all face on a daily basis?

15. Do you waste a lot of emotional energy trying to change or "fix" other people? Or have you begun to experience the inner peace that comes from detaching yourself and "releasing" others with love?

16. When life's happenings seem unfair and even cruel, do you tend to fall apart and retreat into self-pity? Or are you gaining acceptance and peace of mind in the belief that each event and seeming adversity has its place in God's larger order?

17. Do you still tend to rely solely on your own devices? Or, in the interest of security and serenity, are you learning to seek strength and guidance from God?

18. Have you been frustrated in your efforts to conceptualize God? Or are you becoming willing to accept His loving presence on faith alone?

19. Do you pray and meditate only when you have a problem? Or are you trying to deepen the channel between yourself and God by communicating with Him regularly, during good times as well as rough ones?

20. Think back to the last time you "did battle" with another person or institution. Try to

remember your emotional state afterward. Was it worth the price?

21. Do you consider surrender a cowardly approach to life's problems? Or is experience showing you that it takes courage and maturity to surrender?

22. Do you still think that there are certain problems too insignificant for God's attention or too important to turn loose?

23. Have you begun to recognize fear's disguises in your life? Are you becoming aware that emotions such as jealousy, anger, and impatience are not always what they appear to be?

24. Are you discovering that fear quickly loses much of its power to harm you when you acknowledge and express it?

25. Are you beginning to put aside your fear of change, and to see that without change there can be no growth?

26. Does fear still have the power to stop you in your tracks? Or are you learning that fear diminishes as faith grows?

27. Do you spend a lot of time rehashing past behavior and experiences—wrongs committed *by* you or *against* you? Or have you begun to take actions to become rid of your resentments, your guilt, your painful secrets?

28. Are you beginning to see, from personal experience, that lingering resentments and guilt cause not only emotional distress but actual physical illness?

29. Are you hanging on to a particular resentment because the wrong committed against you is "unforgivable"? Or have you become convinced that you must let go of *all* your resentments, no matter how justified they seem?

30. Have you witnessed the healing power and experienced the personal freedom that comes from forgiveness?

31. Are you allowing still more excess baggage to accumulate by putting things off, by glossing over mistakes, or by stuffing painful emotions? Or have you begun to deal with these issues on a daily basis before they become burdensome?

32. If you are still looking for the "right" partner or spouse, is it possible that what you are really looking for is someone who will meet your expectations and fill your needs?

33. Do you generally accept people as they are? Or do you tend to see them as fits or misfits of *your* standards and expectations?

34. Do you still have a need to be "better than"—to look good at the expense of others? Or

are you learning that you are truly praiseworthy when you are superior to your previous self?

35. Do you keep feelings bottled up, or leave things unsaid, to avoid "making waves"? Or are you finding that successful communications require a willingness to put yourself on the line by sharing your true feelings and opinions?

36. Are you gradually becoming more comfortable with yourself, not only when you are with other people but when you are alone?

37. Have you discovered the remedy for painful and chronic self-judgment? Are you working on self-acceptance?

38. Are you learning how to temporarily retreat from daily concerns and to recharge yourself? Or is it still your feeling that you don't have time for self-renewal activities?

39. Are you finding ways to function in a sometimes chaotic world with an abiding sense of inner calm?

40. Following your period of meditation, do you carry the stillness with you?

41. Are you learning to channel your mind's incredible power into such life-enhancing pursuits as self-healing, stress reduction, and goal fulfillment?

42. Have you begun to trust your inner voice and to follow its urgings? Are you becoming more spontaneous and creative?

43. Do you tend to view just about everything that happens in terms of how it will affect you? Or are you learning to consider other people's needs and concerns?

44. Do you make a "big deal" out of everything, no matter how truly insignificant it is? Or are you taking yourself less seriously these days and going along with life's flow?

45. Are you learning to spot self-pity when it builds up, and quickly taking actions to become rid of it?

46. As you become increasingly self-aware, are you making the choices and taking the actions that lead to change and inner peace?

47. Is service to others becoming an ever-brighter spot in your life? Have you come to understand, from your own actions, that giving means getting?

Index

ABOUT THE AUTHOR

The author of *Tranquility* chooses to remain anonymous, a practice consistent with recovery program philosophy. He has written several successful books with a combined total of more than one and a quarter million copies in print, including *A Day at a Time*, a classic work in recovery literature, *A New Day, A Time to Be Free*, and *At My Best*.